M000309758

IT TAKES FIVE TO TANGO

Published by Grammar Factory Publishing, an imprint of MacMillan Company Limited.

Grammar Factory Publishing
MacMillan Company Limited
25 Telegram Mews, 39th Floor, Suite 3906
Toronto, Ontario, Canada
M5V 3Z1

www.grammarfactory.com

Voelter, Verena
    It Takes Five to Tango: From competition to cooperation in health care / Verena Voelter, MD.

Paperback ISBN 978-1-989737-31-6
Hardcover ISBN 978-1-989737-32-3
eBook ISBN 978-1-989737-33-0

    1. BUS010170 BUSINESS & ECONOMICS / Industries / Healthcare. 2. MED036000 MEDICAL / Health Policy. 3. BUS070130 BUSINESS & ECONOMICS / Industries / Pharmaceuticals & Biotechnology.

Production Credits
Cover design by Designerbility
Interior layout design by Dania Zafar
Book production and editorial services by Grammar Factory Publishing

Grammar Factory's Carbon Neutral Publishing Commitment
From January 1st, 2020 onwards, Grammar Factory Publishing is proud to be neutralizing the carbon footprint of all printed copies of its authors' books printed by or ordered directly through Grammar Factory or its affiliated companies through the purchase of Gold Standard-Certified International Offsets.

IT TAKES FIVE TO TANGO

From Competition To Cooperation in Health Care

VERENA VOELTER, MD

TESTIMONIALS

In a *Tango for Five*, Dr Verena Voelter offers two fundamental reframes that will be critical in solving the American healthcare dilemma. First – the notion that we must include multiple perspectives and include the clinical, professional, policy and business lens – with the patient/consumer perspective being the primary one. Second – the notion that we need to reframe the relationships amongst the stakeholders, shifting from a competitive, isolating stance to a more collaborative, co-creative dance. I love the adoption of the metaphor of the Tango that Verena introduces us to. We – all of the various stakeholders in health care – need to join in this new dance and contribute to a whole that is far greater – not far lesser – than the sum of its parts. We need to Tango.

Zeev Neuwirth, MD, Chief Clinical Executive Atrium Health,
Author of 'Reframing Healthcare', US

In my 40 years of collaborative negotiation work world-wide in health care, I have often wanted to assemble the key stakeholders to devise a better approach. The major missing element has been a common vision of success. In this book, Dr Voelter has framed that vision and offers a process for its implementation. We have a lot of productive work ahead thanks to her insights.

Charles L Barker, LLM,
Managing Director of Prime Mover Associates, US

In her provocative and inspiring book, Dr Voelter weaves the fabric of health care: the interconnectivity of the five main decision makers – patients, pharma, payers, policy, providers – and how we can learn and understand the challenges ahead. More importantly, what we need to do to switch our incentive structure and how we can learn to offer a customer-focused solution. Her deep understanding of the health care industry – both from the perspective of an oncologist and pharmaceutical industry leader – offers unparalleled insights into the complexities of the problems we face, yet at the same time, it offers practical solutions.

This is the first integrative book of its kind and will likely be a standard in the field.

Maciej Lesniak, MD, Professor and Chair, Department of Neurological Surgery, Northwestern University, Feinberg School of Medicine, US

As a patient for many decades, I thoroughly and warmly welcome Dr Voelter's insightful and visionary drive for a much-needed reform in health care. She outlines what's needed for the future: moving from reactivity to proactivity through collaboration, trust and empowerment. The book delivers tangible advice – backed by both science and personal experience – making it a must-read for anyone who is involved in health care in any capacity. Let's dance!

Hanna Boëthius, Diabetes Patient Expert and Founder at the Low Carb Universe, Switzerland

Through her research lens, and her focus on patients as a physician, Dr Voelter has written a passionate plea for reform in health care. Her experience as a founder and successful business leader reinforced her belief that cooperation in this complex ecosystem is a prerequisite for long-lasting success. She doesn't tap dance around the basic purpose: improving clinical outcomes at affordable rates. Through plenty of lively examples from her own experience, she puts the possible solutions into the context of the COVID-19 pandemic. This book is a must-read for all those who feel compelled to change the course towards a value-based health care system.

Philippe van Holle, Former President Celgene International, Switzerland

Dr Voelter provides an excellent framework and outline of what needs to happen for the health care quandary to be addressed successfully for all involved – especially patients! And, all 5Ps have to play their role to break down the bureaucracy and contribute value.

Nakisa Serry, JD, LLM, MBA, General Counsel Galderma, Switzerland

Health care as we used to know it, mostly centered around the doctor, is gone. Among other factors, the empowerment of health consumers, the emergence of digital technologies and the COVID-19 crisis have accelerated its transformation. We have now clearly entered a patient-centered, technology-powered, value-based era. Dr Voelter, in this landmark book, not only perfectly describes this ongoing evolution, she also makes it clear – through very convincing conceptualization, powerful illustration and ample stories of her own – what will make our systems more efficient in this new normal: the five key stakeholders – the 5Ps – learning to work (and dance!) together. For good.

**Pascal Deschaseaux, MD,
CEO NewClin and GM Institut Carnot OPALE, France**

The name of Dr Voelter's book captures the essentials. She writes: "*In my thirty year career in this industry, everyone whom I have encountered – be it in the public health sector or in the private life sciences sector – has chosen to work here for a reason*". Oh Yes, that is exactly it. We have a shared mission and it's time to focus more on cooperation around that mission. It Takes Five to Tango!

Verena writes eloquently from her own extensive experience and charts a compelling path forward: a path that is guided by great real-life examples and sharp research and analysis.

I can wholeheartedly recommend this book to anyone who feels passionate about improving health care.

Paavo Perttula, CEO and Founder at Gesund Partners, Finland

Dr Voelter provides a clear analysis of the shortcomings in our health care systems that became so apparent during the COVID-19 pandemic. These issues are inherent flaws in the current systems. Policymakers play an important strategic role to design a holistic framework that is the basis for re-setting our systems. The focus must be to bring important and sustainable value to society. This can only be done in close cooperation among the various actors patients, payers, pharmaceutical industry and academia – using neutral platforms such as public-private partnerships.

Katrin Rupalla, PharmD, PhD, MBA,
SVP Head Regulatory Lundbeck, Denmark

The complexity and interconnectivity of the health care sector require a holistic approach of all actors – with patient centricity and sustainable patient empowerment as the centerpiece to a resilient system. But how can we further develop our systems in a future-oriented way and overcome the existing hurdles? With her excellent book, Dr Voelter provides a purpose-based path to make health care more innovative, smarter, faster and more efficient. Now is time for all actors to act and to dance – together!

Ilka Dekan, CFO AOK Plus, Germany

The challenges of health care – access, affordability, equity, and the need to motivate and reward innovation – are daunting, and the stakes are literally life and death. Dr Voelter's book could not be more timely. She makes a compelling case for enhanced coordination and collaboration among the multiple players comprising the health care ecosystem and offers practical advice for transformational change.

Jonathan Hughes, Partner at Vantage Partners, US

To Roger, my tango partner in life.

Contents

ABOUT THE AUTHOR

 Dr Verena Voelter is a passionate oncologist and experienced business leader. With over twenty-five years' experience at the forefront of health care, she has held key positions as an attending clinician researcher in the hospital setting, and as an executive leader in small and large biotech pharmaceutical companies across three continents: Europe, Asia and the United States. With her unique views on both the public and private sectors, she strongly believes in collaboration as the key to unlock the quandary in health care among patients, providers, pharma, payers and policymakers. Today, she brings credibility as a neutral mediator, executive coach and teacher to the benefit of all stakeholders, both as the founder of 5P Health Care Solutions® as well as an Adjunct Professor for Kellogg's Public-Private Interface Initiative at Northwestern University in Chicago. Since she first outlined the *Tango for Five* concept, Verena has felt encouraged by the early feedback to continue sharing her stories and experiences in order to motivate others. This book is for all who wish to be part of the solution rather than part of the problem. Change in worldwide health care is possible once we dance it together as a *Tango for Five* – as you shall soon see in this book. Verena is curious to hear from you and reachable on her blog **TangoForFive.com.** Follow what's new on the website **5PHealthCareSolutions.com** and on Twitter **@5PHCS.**

FOREWORD

When I first received Dr Voelter's manuscript, I was struck with the power and timeliness of her message to foster cooperation between various stakeholders with a unity of purpose: improving patients' health at affordable costs. We spend a huge chunk of our public spending on health. The question can be asked: is our dollar, franc or euro well spent and are we making the right choices? Verena pushes the reset button while the iron is hot – during a pandemic.

What needs to happen to reconnect the dots and heal our ailing system? This core question invades Verena's critical mind as a researcher, physician, professor, founder and successful business leader. This book is about solutions, not about gerrymandering stakeholders' responsibilities. She tackles the backbreaking burden on her fellow physicians, inadequate health care systems particularly highlighted as a result of COVID-19, and the inverse relationship between costs and quality of care. Why haven't we cracked the code in this nascent Fourth Industrial Revolution?

This book highlights the fundamental lack of connectedness among the top five actors in health care to drive transformational instead of incremental change.

One of the merits of this book is outlining the five stakeholders in almost all of the health decisions we make: patients, providers, pharma, payers and policymakers. However, due to conflicting agendas, there is a disconnect between these five stakeholders. According to Verena, we all came to health care for a reason: to care for patients and create value within the system by working together to create new health care solutions. What unites us is a strong, genuine sense of purpose. So, what needs to change?

Firstly, there are multiple conflicts of interest between the private and public health care sectors that need to be addressed. Then, we need to embrace the advent of the digitally advanced, smart policymaker, looking at those issues with a long-term objective. Unfortunately, that is one of the reasons why the health care engine sputters regularly. We face a constant dilemma between the short-term incentives behind our actions and the actual, long-term impact of our actions. Further, our democratic system requires politicians to concentrate too often on (re)election and therefore the immediate impact overtakes any long-term consideration. We need to find ways to depoliticize health care and allow experts to focus on what they know to do best: develop, deliver and drive health care to patients.

Lack of progress in health care has not been for lack of trying. However, efforts to reduce costs, to improve policy and to address quality have remained a tinkering at the edges (figure i).

This book not only explores the responsibility of the patient, the importance of health literacy and the clinical components of health, but also outlines the

social determinants of health, such as behavioral
components and the importance of education.

It showcases how the digital revolution in health care brings not only better coordination and restores efficiencies among the health care actors, but also holds great promise to empower patients and bring a greater level of cooperation in what today is an imbalance of bargaining power, with the patient being the weakest part in the value chain. Verena reminds us of the essence of health care: the empowerment of the patient and patient centricity in all we do along the value chain. Personally, I had to first retire before I started to visit my doctor and seriously take care of my own health. Our busy lives don't always allow us to look after our body with all its limitations. Education is an essential factor here – from secondary school onwards. We learn history, geography and philosophy from a young age, but nobody can remember any school lesson about how to better care for our health (which involves not only diet and exercise, but also work-life balance). We get diplomas for entering the labor market, but we are illiterate when it comes to managing our body's lifecycle.

One example: in the United Kingdom, childhood obesity costs the National Institute for Health Research (NIHR) $7.9 billion and wider society about $35 billion (or about four percent of UK National Health Service [NHS] budget and a much higher share of the health care budget due to direct medical costs), according to findings published by the National Audit Office in September 2020.[1] Some argue that school food is to blame. Probably so. However, I would go for an awareness campaign at schools, through creative and funny exercise-focused health apps, and sponsorship of video game companies to intermingle diet-related messages in their offerings.

Further, today's young generation is the most ecologically and digitally sensitive. That same generation needs to call out the root causes of an out-of-control health issue! The long-term impact on cost reduction in addressing adult obesity, for example, will be exponential. This book is a fantastic introduction for whoever wants to be part of the solution rather than the problem.

Figure i. Past efforts to address health care issues have been tinkering at the edges.

Fundamentally, health care today is suffering from a broken incentives system.

We incentivize volume, not quality. On the provider side, this comes in the form of a fee-for-service (FFS) and diagnosis-related grouping (DRG) system, which classifies services and goods for payment. No link to patient outcomes is foreseen. For providers, hospitals and doctors, such a system is a catch-22 because it rewards quantity of visits, surgeries and prescribed medicines. There is no reward to deliver quality of care. Artificial intelligence and machine learning have to change that equation by collecting patient outcomes data through state-regulated databases from participating providers (membership could be rewarded) and calculate a value-based DRG over a much wider sample. Many places are still miles away from this, but a concerted effort is necessary now. This book lists many examples where coalitions between patients, doctors, hospitals, payers and administrators have seen improved profitability margins. Much better than traditional models ever did, which in turn have been charging too much, receiving public funding, lacking competition, or just filling a supply-demand gap.

Policy-wise, we are confronted with dilemmas. Health care is by far the most global asset, which is why we created the science-based World Health Organization (WHO) to oversee pandemics such as COVID-19 and many other life-threatening diseases. Unfortunately, it didn't turn out like that because global health care became center stage for political debate. Verena rightfully points out the extent of over-politicization of health care and the need to include policy as a proactive factor for optimization. We seem to have this well under control for monetary and fiscal policies, with global organizations such as the International Monetary Fund (IMF), European Central Bank (ECB), World Bank and national banks, which form a well-interconnected web with strong leaders. Why can't we learn about what works in financials, depoliticize health care and adopt those learnings? We need similarly well-operating entities for health care. Verena says, 'Think global, act local.' That is what we need.

Pharma and drug costs represent less than twenty percent of the health care budget in developed countries, as you can read in the first chapter about root causes to our ailing systems. But they contribute far more to the population's life expectancy, and therefore to the global economic output, long term. However, we are facing a crisis of trust – or mistrust – between the five actors and between society and pharma. The book is not dwelling on, nor arguing, this point. It's simply about knowing that there has been abuse of bargaining power and price gouging by a few actors; knowing that there are varying perceptions of how equitable the benefits are; and acknowledging that we are facing an affordability issue.

What is certain, and what this book beautifully carves out, is that finger-pointing and singling out villains is no solution.

Repetitive cycles of investments, scientific discoveries and new patient therapies have saved millions of lives. Particularly in oncology, this business model has worked. However, short-term focus on return-on-investment, in a high-risk, high-cost drug development landscape, is contributing to a broken balance between innovation and affordability. What we need are novel reimbursement schemes and value-based, long-term pricing models that take patient- and population-based impact into account, and that allow risk to be shared over time between private and public. We have seen how this works in light of a global crisis – a vaccine development against SARS-CoV-2 in less than twelve months is unprecedented and only possible due to a high level of cooperation between all actors.

Lastly, value creation is all about improving life expectancy and quality of life. You don't move outcomes if you don't change value. Conversely, improving outcomes via prohibitive costs or over-emphasizing cost initiatives will not move the needle on value (figure ii) if they remain decoupled from impact on patient outcomes, and hence add no value. We should therefore abandon new policies, initiatives and processes that aim at cost reduction solely. We need to minimize actors' costs in the supply chain that do not contribute to improving outcomes. Transporting a medication from A to B is not a value-adding act for better clinical outcomes. Hence this cannot account for large amounts of a health care budget as it is now.

Figure ii. A simple equation for value-based health care (VBHC).

$$\text{Value} = \frac{\text{Outcomes}}{\text{Cost}}$$

Changes are underway among more and more national health agencies leveraging the value-based health care (VBHC) concept. The right incentive for the right amount of health interventions will be based on big data from a wide range of sources – healthy individuals, patients at risk, and those suffering mild to severe conditions – to understand the health continuum from one stage to another, such as the Nordic Health 2030 Movement discussed in chapter three. In Europe, one could imagine that all member states feed into one database, with algorithms helping to decide how to finance a particular health intervention. Smart use of big data will allow for fewer health interventions altogether through better prevention. It is shameful, as Verena concludes, that thirty to fifty percent of health care is considered wasteful. After all, we may have the resources, but they are badly allocated.

The book illustrates a number of successful private-public partnerships. It is true that many health initiatives are in the hands of private enterprises, while others demand a closer alliance between big tech and government agencies. A federal or national D-Health program has tremendous impact on the inverted cost-quality curve. Unfortunately, today these initiatives are fragmented and therefore not eye-opening enough. This book, and particularly its 'digital' chapter four, offers a series of examples and aims to stimulate a culture of best-practice sharing.

Let me conclude by comparing health care to a sparkling diamond, caused by light reflections of its unique shape. Each facet of the diamond represents a different stakeholder within health care. The clarity of the diamond is the degree of cooperation with which we build the health care options of tomorrow, creating win-wins for all actors. The owner of the diamond is the patient who neglects too often to take care of it, or in many cases is not insured enough when the diamond is damaged or stolen.

We have a long way to go, but the tools to restore the balance between innovation and affordability are all here. All we have to do is apply them. Individually. Collectively.

All of the necessary tools are outlined in this book. I applaud Verena for her courage to bring facets of all actors to the surface. This book is a must-read for anybody who wants to be part of fixing our systems, but has been wondering how to do it. It is the recipe for how we all better tango in health care: patients, providers, pharma, payers and policy.

Philippe van Holle,
Former president of Celgene International

PREFACE

"The purpose of human life is to serve, and to show compassion and the will to help others."

~ DR ALBERT SCHWEITZER

WHY I WROTE THIS BOOK

I deeply, deeply care for patients. It is in my guts; it is in my body and in my soul. I was eight years old when I first entered a hospital lobby with my aunty in the Black Forest in Germany. She was a children's nurse, working on the newborn ward. Convinced that I'd be thrilled to see the newborn babies, she decided to bring me along to work. What she did not foresee, though, was that this would be a decisive day, determining the rest of my life. I decided to become a doctor.

I can still see that hospital door swing open and, appearing behind a large lobby, silent people were wandering around. Some were wearing white coats with buttons down the front, while others were wearing white coats buttoned at the back. Only later would I understand that the former were doctors, and the latter patients. What I remember to this day is the smell. I cannot tell you what it was. What I can tell you, though, is that I still have the same sensation when entering a hospital to this day. It is a feeling of belonging and connection. With patients. With doctors.

Years later, during my studies at medical school, I came across the memoirs of Dr Albert Schweitzer, a visionary theologian, musician and physician. Born some 100 years earlier in the Alsatian mountains west of the Black Forest, he would become one of the guiding role models for my own career. As a holistic caregiver, he would consider someone's body *and* soul, and looked at medicine as a hybrid of art and science. It's no wonder he received the Nobel Peace Prize for his philosophy of "Reverence for Life". In his book of the same name, he described his medical work in Africa. As a man of empathy, curiosity and action, he put his theoretical considerations into practice. At the beginning of the twentieth century, he and his wife founded the hospital Lambarene in Gabon, where he treated patients with a focus on advancing the study and care of leprosy and malaria.

After many years at the forefront of medicine myself, I feel fortunate for the rich experiences and encounters I have had as a passionate doctor in internal medicine and oncology, and as a dedicated business leader in the pharmaceutical industry. I have seen first-hand the phenomenal progress in science that has helped so many patients.

I have witnessed the power of collaboration between passionate researchers in the clinics and in the pharmaceutical industry.

I have been part of co-creating groundbreaking new solutions when doctors, patients and pharma come together with payers and policymakers. I have seen it in Europe, in Asia, and in the United States.

However, 100 years after Dr Schweitzer pioneered the principles of holistic medicine, our systems of health are largely broken. Based on the wrong incentives, the great progress made in medicine is now hitting a ceiling of affordability and inequality.

WHY I AM WRITING THIS BOOK NOW

Reflecting on three decades in health care, I have been wondering, "What needs to happen to reconnect the dots and heal our ailing systems?" What needs to happen for people to realize that health care is not just a commodity? What needs to happen for society to realize that physicians and nurses are not machines or visit vendors? What needs to happen for us to start putting the same value tag on *care* that we do on innovation, procedures and technology? For too long, the dialogue seemed to be dominated by finger-pointing, and distrust was at an all-time high, when suddenly a global, cataclysmic event happened.

In 2020, the universe decided that health care is THE most important thing.

Everyone now realizes how deeply health care is woven into the fabric of our societies. The SARS-CoV-2 virus has been wreaking havoc on our health care systems (figure iii). Everyone experiences the shortcomings, outdated infrastructures and slow processes in a health care system that is managed by a set of disconnected solo dancers with a silo-like mentality. Everyone starts to see the vast complexity of this industry and some start realizing that it's not possible for one single actor to be solely responsible for the solution.

Figure iii. SARS-CoV-2 wreaking havoc on health care systems.

Meanwhile, when people were dying by the masses in Italy and New York City in the spring of 2020, as many hospitals struggled to supply the most basic equipment, health care workers became the heroes of the year. However, during the second wave the following winter, a lack of technical equipment was no longer causing a bottleneck. Ventilators, intensive care beds and hospital capacity were proactively managed. But what good is this when hospital staff are exhausted and burnt out, and no one is left to run the machines and care for the patients?

Health care is not a commodity. It is a central pillar in our societies. If we want to value our health, we need to value all parts of the health care chain equally.

Today, more than ever, I feel for my fellow physicians and the backbreaking burden they carry. I worry for our health care systems, which are collapsing under an upward cost spiral and a loss of quality in care in an already chaotic world. I worry that we may definitely lose the grip on progress in medicine if we do not push the reset button. There is no better time to reset it than in the middle of a pandemic. History has shown that crises forge renewal, as they force us to change. We know that change does not come without loss. But in 2020, loss came regardless. So let's look at it from the perspective of the uphill slope out of the crisis: we are at an inflection point in health care and the good news is that there are solutions. I firmly believe that amid all the disruption and uncertainty, we are holding a precious diamond for renewal in our hands. Further encouraged by the landmark books published in recent years by my fellow physicians, Dr Ezekiel Emanuel (*Which Country Has the World's Best Health Care?*) and Dr Zeev Neuwirth (*Reframing Health Care: A Roadmap for Creating Disruptive Change*), I knew it was the right time for me to share my stories, observations and thoughts for change.[2,3]

We can now renew our commitment to what the primary purpose of health care is: serving the patient, fighting illnesses and protecting health. Therefore, we all need to take ownership: patients, providers, pharma, payers and policymakers, together in a Tango for Five.

I have been fortunate enough to see many pilot projects in value-based health care, digitalization and multi-party collaboration come to fruition. What they now need is showcasing, sharing and perpetuating at scale. This is why I am writing this book. It is a book of encouragement and not of complaints. It is intended for all patients and health care professionals who are curious to learn more about what these pilot projects hold, and what everyone can do to move the needle in health care.

Curious to hear how to possibly solve this quandary and what *you* can do to help solve it? I invite you to dance with me in the *Tango for Five*.

Verena

Prioritizing health care for the benefit of our economies and societies

"This is the nature of emergencies. They fast-forward historical processes."

~ YUVAL NOAH HARARI

HEALTH CARE IS EVERYONE'S RESPONSIBILITY

When I started writing this book, a single virus had brought the whole world to a standstill. As I stated in the preface, it highlighted how intimately health care is woven into the fabric of our societies, including our economies and livelihoods. Within the first two months of the pandemic, over twenty million people lost their jobs in the US alone, with a majority of these people also failing to maintain their health care coverage.[4] Very quickly, it became evident that health care is not only about clinical features, but that social determinants of health have an overwhelming impact on our lives. In Chicago, where I am teaching pharmaceutical strategy at Northwestern University's Kellogg School of Management, a recent report documented the striking disparities.[5] The risk of dying from COVID-19 is almost four times higher for African-Americans than for whites, accounting for fifty-six percent versus 15.8 percent of all deaths. This is in stark contrast to the racial make-up of the city, which stands at thirty percent and thirty-three percent respectively.

Health care is both very personal and at the same time globally interconnected.

This virus did not know borders and did not travel with a passport. It did not discriminate between rich and poor, between East and West. It has shown us that we have to work together and break down barriers of collaboration, both real and perceived.

Yes, our health care systems were seriously broken long before the pandemic hit. We are facing a range of issues, including unsustainable costs, poor outcomes, distrust, and frustrated actors, all throughout the ecosystem (patients, doctors, payers, regulators, politicians, pharma and the life sciences sector). But somehow, people may have been thinking that health care is this complicated and specialized "thing" on the side. That it's something they hopefully "never need to deal with", or that it's so broken that "anyway, there is nothing I can do to fix it."

This pandemic has proven us wrong on both counts. It touches all of us. And there is a way to fix it – through collaborative partnerships across the public and the private sectors.

No single root cause, no single actor alone, is responsible for the issues that are plaguing our systems of health.

WHY IT TAKES MORE THAN "TWO TO TANGO"

During a virtual think tank conference, I stumbled over an eye-opening concept that I immediately knew would become the guiding theme for this book and for the way I look at solution-building for our health care problems in general.

Pablo Pugliese is a renowned tango dancer who has been dancing tango all his life, and who created a leadership institute based on tango principles (I invite you to explore his website).[6] The particular aspect of tango he brings to his leadership training is the fact that there is no clearly defined set of rules and steps that govern a tango, making it unlike other dances such as a waltz or a cha-cha-cha. Instead, there is a set of *common vocabulary*, or principles, that both dancers use to communicate. Furthermore, what Pablo and his partner Noel exemplify perfectly is the fact that there is no one constant or dominant leader. Both partners can slip into the leader role at any time, without competition, and swap responsibility for the lead back and forth.

By learning a common vocabulary, and by co-owning leadership, both partners co-create innovative new dances every time they get on stage.

In health care, it is even more complex. To solve a problem, it takes not two to tango, but five. If you think about it, it all starts and ends with the patient. Patients receiving care, doctors delivering care, pharma developing care, payers paying for care, and policymakers providing the ethical and regulatory frameworks for the health care delivery chain. Principles instead of rules, and cooperation instead of competition. How true is this in health care? Among the top five actors – patient, provider, pharma, payer and policymaker – no one is the boss. Every actor is highly interconnected on every step along the way. All are equitable leaders who have to co-create solutions in a fair manner, and constantly communicate in a dance that juggles all actors, interests and needs.

Figure iv. From fragmentation to coordination in health care.

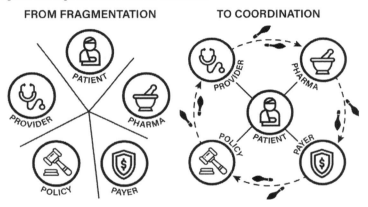

However, in today's reality, these top five actors rarely conceive themselves as part of one entity or industry with accountability to one another. Unfortunately, they can even see themselves as antagonists, sparring in conflict, or worse, they can pass the accountability 'down' to the patient. What would it take for the five decision makers to feel connected and behave as members of one and the same enterprise or industry, with accountability to one another in the service of the patient?

Truth be told, only a holistic effort between providers, patients and payers, as well as the pharmaceutical industry and policymakers, will be able to overcome the herculean task of healing our ailing systems and allowing us to move from a fragmented, silo mentality to coordination in a *Tango for Five* (figure iv).

Health care is not a solo-dancing show; it is not even a tango for two. Instead, it comprises all five main decision makers in health care in an interconnected Tango for Five.

In light of this unprecedented pandemic, breakthrough innovation was possible through an unheard-of coalition of public and private members within the health care ecosystem. Multiple pharmaceutical companies, as well as the US Food and Drug Administration (FDA), European Medicines Agency (EMA), and institutions such as the National Institutes of Health (NIH) in the US and the World Health Organization (WHO), have rallied to develop a series of novel approaches to fighting this virus in astronomically record time – *together*. What usually takes several years, or decades, has been accomplished in under a year.

In light of a crisis, when stakes are high, collaboration works. Even in health care.

However, even outside of a crisis, we should be doing better. Much better. The tools are all there – all we need to do is apply them. Scholars and practitioners have long agreed that a shift from transactional FFS systems toward a patient-centric system that rewards outcomes and quality of care, usually referred to as value-based health care (VBHC), is the way to go. Other industries have long recognized that a renewed focus on the consumer and the customer experience yields far better business outcomes than only focusing on selling products. Isn't this ironic? Shouldn't health care be all about its ultimate customer, the patient?

Somehow, health care is late to this show. (As you shall see in the next chapters.) In many ways, we have to fix the plane while we fly it. And we have to modernize it at the same time.

This requires a fundamental culture change, with leaders adopting new sets of skills. Gone are the days when a doctor could tell a patient in a patronizing way what treatment to choose. Gone are the days when we could afford to waste resources on lengthy hospital stays and lingering, sequential drug development cycles. Gone are the days when government and payer pockets were deep enough to pay for every new pill and invention in medicine. Gone are the days when we could operate with paper charts and fax machines. We don't have that time and money anymore.

If we don't change, the system will crack. We will not be able to pay for it any longer – not for innovation and not for care. But finding the solution by focusing on each actor in isolation won't be successful in what is a highly interconnected health care ecosystem.

WHAT YOU CAN EXPECT FROM THIS BOOK AND HOW IT IS ORGANIZED

Now is the time to think big and harness the momentum of the disruption caused by COVID-19. We can only conceive complexity when it becomes personal. This is what I feel is different now. Transforming health care and systems is not easy; it takes time and the problem is so big that it can be intimidating. However, one of the upsides of the pandemic is that it has shown that change is possible. What you'll find in the following chapters are tools and principles that demonstrate that those who decide to be part of the solution can have an impact. By switching from competing in a solo dance to cooperating within a *Tango for Five*, we have a true opportunity to make long-lasting change for the benefit of ourselves, our beloved ones and future generations.

Figure v. What to expect from the book – Part I: learn, Part II: do.

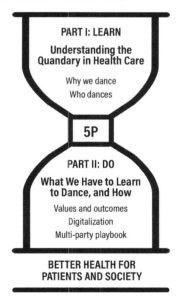

PART I of this book is all about learning and understanding the problem. In order words, *why* we need to change and *who* needs to change (figure v).

If we want to overcome the quandary in health care, we need to truly understand what's broken. The public narrative is wrongly focused on trying to identify who's to blame and is generally lacking imagination on what is feasible. Gaining a deep understanding of who the main actors are, and how their interdependency plays into the root causes of our ailing health care systems, can be enlightening as we seek to identify and co-create novel solutions in order to restore, or replace, what's broken.

Getting the facts right is paramount. Therefore, chapter one analyzes the drivers of our health care expenditure, pinpoints the root causes of our wasteful care delivery, and explores where opportunities for change may lie.

Chapter two focuses on the realities, pressures and objectives that lie behind deeply rooted feelings of frustration, which seem to be so common within the health care ecosystem. But rarely are the various actors aware of the others' frustrations. And often, the reasons for these frustrations are as diverse as the actors themselves. In order to make substantial progress in solving the issues at hand, we must work together. However, we cannot work together if we do not trust each other. Rebuilding trust and forging connections between people starts with understanding and knowing the people behind the problems.

Once we have a full picture of the root causes, we can turn to action.

Part II is about doing and action. Specifically, *what* we need to do to radically switch our incentive structure and *how* we can learn to effectively dance a *Tango for Five* in a fair, sustainable and equitable manner. In brief, everything starts with the customer. A solution that isn't customer-focused is a wasted and useless solution. In health care, the ultimate customer is the patient.

The core ingredients for change are already well known and available, so we do not even have to waste time inventing them. That is the good news – ample pilot projects are already underway globally in the following three areas: applying the principles of patient-centered VBHC (chapter three); acquiring the digital toolbox of the Fourth Industrial Revolution (chapter four); and adopting a playbook to effectively orchestrate the multi-party collaboration required between the top five actors in health care: patients, providers, pharma, payers and policymakers (chapter five).

I have personally witnessed the power of all three areas to move the needle on health care. The aim of this book is to share experiences and real-life scenarios, demonstrating how cooperation in health care holds true transformative power to bring us better health outcomes for patients and society more broadly.

PART I

LEARN

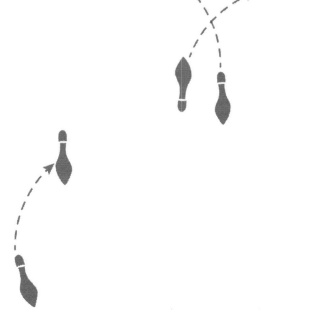

CHAPTER 1

Restoring the broken balance between innovation and affordability

*"It is health that is real wealth and
not pieces of gold and silver."*

~ MAHATMA GANDHI

A QUICK FIX, BUT AT WHAT COST?

"Verena, you should run a 'big lab' on this patient," was the first thing I recall my supervising attending physician shouting across the corridor. In the mid-1990s, I had just started on the internal medicine ward in a mid-size hospital in rural Germany, solely responsible for twenty-six patients with conditions ranging from myocardial insufficiency and hepatic failure to wound healing issues from a complication of diabetes called "the diabetes leg". Fresh out of medical school a couple of months earlier, much of this felt like a foreign language despite what I had learned on the benches of my universities in Bonn, Lausanne and Strasbourg.

These were the years when resources and the quest for finances were not part of the vocabulary we would learn as students or medical residents. Looking back, I realize that much of the culture back then was to first run a bunch of tests, exams and radiology imaging to see whether we could find anything abnormal in the results, rather than talking to the patient first and reflecting, "What is it that I am actually looking for?" Then, tailoring the requested lab exams accordingly. Big lab versus small was a distinction never made. It was so much easier to use the pre-filled big lab sheet, which had every single line item ticked off, than having to think which test to ask for and filling it in manually in the small lab version, and thinking about how much all of this costs.

Testing first. Thinking second. That has become the culture in the medical arena.

Fast-forward thirty years to the start of 2020, just before the pandemic hit, I came across an eye-opening article in the *ASH Clinical News* (for members of the American Society of Clinical Hematology).[7] "*As physicians, we've been trained to test, test, test. We are, I think, appropriately concerned about missing things, but that culture can lead to harms from overtesting,*" recounts Dr Lisa Hicks, Chair of the ASH's committee on quality. I was astonished, and felt ashamed at the same time, to see that so little had changed and that I had been just as much a part of this culture as anybody else. Overtesting can lead to cost for the system and to harm for the patient.

Today, however, we cannot afford to perpetuate this culture any longer. We need to radically shift our mindsets and medical education to first ask: "What possible disease may this patient be suffering from?" And then only demand lab tests and imaging exams that help to discard or confirm our hypothesis.

Both the public and the experts are part of the trend
that prioritizes technical procedures over primary care.

It seems to have become common practice to take a pill, available to us twenty-four hours a day, seven days a week, for everything – a vitamin pill, a happy pill, a sleeping pill and so on – in addition to remedies for all our other illnesses, such as high blood pressure, diabetes, high cholesterol and more. We seem to have lost the sense of what is essential versus what is nice to have. We also have lost the sense of what we can fix with a pill versus what we can do by changing our behaviors, lifestyle choices, and environment (both at home and at work), as illustrated in figure 1.1.

Figure 1.1. Our culture: a pill for everything.

We are facing a crisis of waste in health care. We should only test, treat and provide therapy when we need to. Waste and mindful use of resources has become a general theme in our societies, be it in relation to saving energy, lowering carbon emissions or reducing plastic use. Fueled by a generation break, the Millennial generation and generation Z are pushing hard on what is commonly referred to as a "circular economy". Nature doesn't know waste. In 2020, Greta Thunberg, founder of the worldwide initiative "Fridays for Future", tweeted the following on Black Friday, right before Thanksgiving: *"Don't buy stuff you don't need."*[8] When I read this over my morning coffee, I thought to myself, "The same rule applies in health care."

Today, we are running health care like a body shop for cars. Fixing and reacting with a pill for everything, instead of fostering prevention, self-empowerment and lifestyle changes.

THE BROKEN BALANCE

Fundamentally, everyone agrees that health care today is built on the wrong incentives. If you incentivize action, pills and procedures, what you get is an expectation of action, pills and procedures. All it does is drive costs up. There is no incentive built in for doing "nothing", for doing less or for changing behaviors; not for patients, not for providers, not for pharma, not for payers. However, in today's world, resources are limited, and so we can no longer afford to waste dollars and energy.

Because resources are limited, actors are competing over bargaining power and are shifting cost burdens, and responsibility for the broken system, to each other.

As a result, divides are deepening and costs are rising. Amid all of this complexity and uncertainty surrounding who holds the ultimate decision-making power, one thing is certain: the patient is always losing out. When I look at the image in figure 1.2, I am reminded of the disconnected patient (the single pebble on the right), hanging up in the air while the four other constituents hold all the bargaining power, probably in this descending order: pharma, payer, provider, policy. I am also thinking of the imbalance between innovation and affordability, with innovation hanging up in the air, wondering who will pay for it, while the heavy burden of affordability weighs down the other side.

Figure 1.2. The imbalance in health care.

Today, with its laser focus on quantity, the FFS system is quality agnostic. There is no built-in incentive that measures how well a patient is doing after a procedure or a treatment, in either the medium or long term. In the case of a hip replacement, for example, only the hip replacement itself is paid for; there is no built-in incentive for patients feeling better and actually being able to walk again three or six months later. Rewards for value, and what matters to patients, are not part of that equation. Similarly, no rewards are given to patients and providers if they foster lifestyle and behavioral changes. So everyone is trapped in this vicious circle of delivering pills and services for money.

It has not been for a lack of trying to fix the system, though.

In an attempt to contain the cost explosion, many countries replaced the FFS with a DRG system. This is intended to regroup similar diseases, payment formulas and clinical outcomes, but it does not alter the underlying incentive system and still favors the selling of services without an incentive link to patient outcomes.[9] As a consequence, many places introduced budgets caps, which has not moved the needle on affordability either, because the rewards on volume have not changed.

In an FFS system, those doctors who do less and spend more time with patients, trying to do the right thing for them, are being severely penalized.

This creates a disastrous situation filled with frustration, distrust and resource constraints, leaving little room for constructive dialogue between the actors.

Overall, let's be clear. The progress in science and medicine has led to a steep rise in life expectancy over the past 100 years. However, these gains in longevity have actually started to take a reverse trend. Despite increasing health care budgets, life expectancy gains have stalled over the past decade. The year 2015 was particularly bad, with life expectancy falling in nineteen countries. This is the first time this has happened since 1970. As shown in the flattening curve of figure 1.3, all the dollars spent on health care for each patient do not translate into longer life expectancy anymore.[10]

Figure 1.3. Life expectancy versus health care spending (per capita) in selected OECD countries.

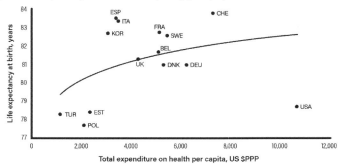

Note: Since only provisional or no data were provided for some countries, the following countries are missing from this graph: Canada, Japan, Mexico and Norway. Source: statsoecd.org.

What does this mean? Let's have a look at a couple of specific numbers.

To give you a concrete order of magnitude, in 2020, for the first time ever, the US surpassed the threshold of $4 trillion in total health care spending (exclusive of COVID-19).[11] It's important to note that health care is the largest industry in the country's economy. In terms of percentage of GDP, it is approaching twenty percent, which is more than double the OECD average, which was 8.8 percent in 2018, and is forecast to grow to ten per cent by 2030.[10] You can spot the outlier dot in the right-hand lower corner of the graph, which shows Americans have an average life expectancy of less than seventy-nine years (compared to the next two countries with the highest health care spending: Switzerland, eighty-three years and Germany, eighty-one years). The US is also the highest in terms of per capita spending, with $10,000 spent per person compared to the OECD average of $4,000 per person.[10]

This exemplifies we are trending toward a breaking point. Societies will not be able to afford health care anymore if radical reforms are not implemented. Even wealthy countries, such as my home country Switzerland, are following that trend, with one out of five people in the lower income percentile paying as much on out-of-pocket expenses and health plan premiums as they do on housing and rent.[2]

Based on this imbalance between dollars spent and longevity gains, the COVID-19 pandemic has shown how disastrous inefficient health care management has been to the overall economy and the fabric of our societies.

In the US alone, due to the COVID-19 pandemic, the economy experienced its steepest ever decline in GDP of -9.1% in the second quarter of 2020. Prior to this, the economy had never experienced a drop of more than 3% since recordkeeping began in 1947.[4]

On a global scale, the importance of health care as an economic sector is even more telling, with one in ten people working in health and social care, as outlined in an OECD report titled "Health at a Glance 2019: OECD Indicators".[10] As such, it is concerning to see that the inefficiency gap continues to grow, with health care spending having long outgrown GDP growth.

So, you may ask: where does all the money go?

Because of the inherent complexity within the health care ecosystem, there is no easy way to determine where all the money goes and why it disappears at such a fast pace. Why is it that we seem to be losing the grip on efficiencies and productivity? Today, we have no means to follow a dollar spent along the value chain from research and development to care delivery and care coordination. The big question is: how can we maintain the virtuous circle of innovation, scientific discovery and progress in medicine while managing the vicious circle of affordability, resources and cost?

Let's have a look at each in more detail.

THE VIRTUOUS CIRCLE

Part of the reason for the inflammatory spotlight on health care is the fact that the global pharmaceutical market is valued at over $1 trillion. This is a tripling in record time; less than twenty years ago, it was valued at just $390 billion.[12] In oncology specifically, a market worth $150 billion was linked to a total mortality decline of twenty-nine percent in the first fifteen years of this millennium, with the sharpest one-year drop ever reported (2.2 percent in 2015).[13,14] As the second leading cause of death worldwide, this impact on cancer care has been massive in terms of public health.[10] Figure 1.4 clearly illustrates this breaking point and the start of mortality decline in the 1990s, coinciding with the rise of the oncology pharmaceutical market. The picture I personally find most compelling is figure 1.5, which shows how the massive investment into cancer research and drug development translates into the number of lives that have been saved from cancer: more than three million people in less than three decades. If you think about it, this is a tangible increase in longevity obtained in less than one generation, which is an unprecedented success in the history of humankind, possibly equaled only by the discovery of penicillin to treat infections and the mortality they cause.

Put another way, a repetitive, virtuous cycle of investments, scientific discoveries and their translation into therapeutic advances has saved millions of lives from cancer.

Figure 1.4. Reduction of cancer-related mortality.

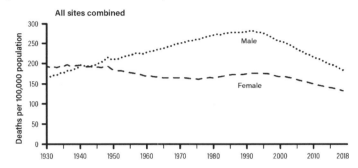

Source: Cancer Statistics 2021 [14]

Figure 1.5. Numbers of averted deaths from cancer.

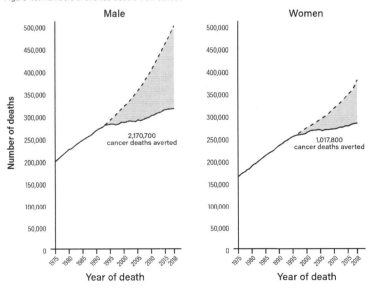

Note: The solid line represents the actual number of cancer deaths recorded in each year; the dashed line represents the number of cancer deaths that would have been expected if cancer rates had remained at their peak.
Source: Cancer Statistics 2021 [14]

Multiple myeloma (MM) is a prime example that showcases the power of such an innovative circle of investments. Considered a "small market" in business terms (just 1.8 percent of new cancer patients are diagnosed with myeloma compared to 14.8 per cent for breast cancer).[15,16] As a result, many analysts would not bookmark this as an appealing area for investment. However, thanks to a couple of visionary physicians and business leaders, in the late 1990s this rare disease grew into one of the most successful and largest markets. Similary to the bending of the curve in figure 1.4, this was reflected in a steep decline in the risk for MM patients of dying from this disease.[17] Within a relatively short period, the median overall survival (OS) doubled from three to five years over the course of two decades to seven to ten years today.[18]

As described in more detail in "The incredible story of thalidomide" (breakout box 1), the unique tragedy of thalidomide was not only the start of the creation of regulatory agencies and dedicated health authorities, such as the FDA and the EMA, around the world, but also the start of a revolution in treating MM patients. In order to optimize side effects such as sleepiness and sensitivity problems, lenalidomide (Revlimid®) had been developed as a second generation in this class of immunomodulatory drugs (IMiDs®).[19,20] This spurred an unprecedented level of investment by pharma and created a number of academic research groups solely focused on MM, such as the Intergroupe Francophone du Myélome (IFM). This collective effort has led to an unprecedented gain in life expectancy for MM patients.[21]

Notably, much of this progress in oncology has not occurred in isolation, by one player, or by one group of the larger health care ecosystem. Be it the progress with targeted therapies in breast cancer, biomarker-directed therapy for lung cancer, immune checkpoint inhibitors for melanoma or monoclonal antibody-enhancing chemotherapy for lymphoma, a tight partnership between academia and the pharmaceutical industry has profoundly contributed to this collective progress.[22-25]

Generations of committed, passionate and incredibly talented researchers on both sides of the spectrum – public academia and private companies alike – have worked together in a highly collaborative fashion.

I will describe examples of these partnerships in more detail in chapters two and five.

As a matter of fact, oncology as a whole has become a highly successful model of innovation, leading to tangible progress for patients, as we have seen. Since the start of the millennium, entire companies have shifted their portfolio and strategy to include oncology, often at the detriment of de-investment in other, less "hot" areas. One of these has been the antibiotics and infectious diseases space, as showcased by a dramatic increase of multi-resistant bacteria, for which no new therapies have been developed in the last thirty years. I will get back to this topic in the next chapter two.

What is weighing heavily on the balance of innovation is the cost and risk of clinical development. Among the "seven hurdles" of drug development, from bench to bedside, did you know that only one substance out of 10,000 to 30,000 molecules in the lab will eventually make it to market as a new product?[26] Furthermore, as depicted in figure 1.6, it takes more than a decade and up to $1 billion to develop one new medicine in one specific indication. Hence, the risk to fail is high.[27] It takes an enormous number of different sets of expertise – from chemists, biologists, toxicologists, clinical pharmacologists, basic researchers and clinician researchers, regulatory experts, commercial forecasting, and pricing and reimbursement experts – to orchestrate this development. This may well be one of the reasons why drug development typically has been covered by the private life sciences sector – because the pockets to cover cost and risks need to be sufficiently deep to make up for the high drop-out rate.

Figure 1.6. The seven hurdles of drug development.

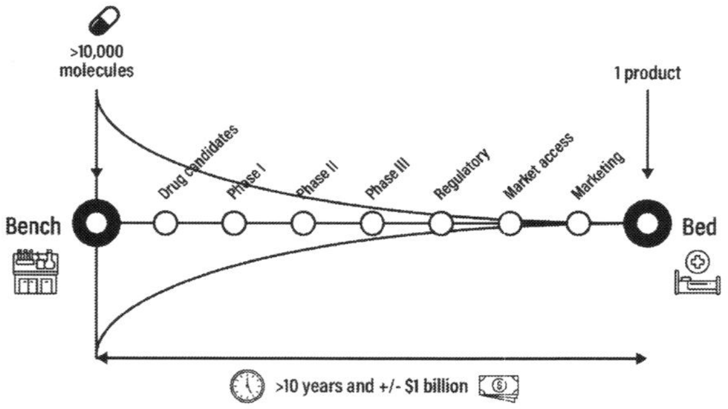

Source: Adapted from Andrew Briggs [26]

Nevertheless, as a whole, oncology has shown that if the incentives to invest and the prospect for viable ROIs are attractive enough, this virtuous circle can produce unprecedented value for patients and society, as showcased in figures 1.4 and 1.5 as a whole and for myeloma in breakout box 1 in particular. Yet, the benefits and the value of these advances are not being perceived as equitable by all parties of the health care ecosystem, nor necessarily by society. Certainly, there are examples where price gouging has occurred, with an unjustifiable clinical value proportional to the net price set.[28] On the other hand, there are equally, if not more, examples where that additional value is clinically meaningful to patients, providers and society, such as breast cancer, lung cancer, melanoma and lymphoma cited earlier.

One thing is certain: no one actor can decide what the right value, price and cost should be. This can only be achieved by a crosstalk between society and experts, or, in other words, between pharma, policy, payers, providers and patients.

BREAKOUT BOX 1: THE INCREDIBLE STORY OF THALIDOMIDE

What started as one of the biggest tragedies in modern medicine eventually turned not only into the instauration of regulatory health authorities globally, but also into one of the success stories in medicine.[29]

In the 1960s the supposedly safe sleeping pill for pregnant women, thalidomide (THAL, branded as Contergan), caused thousands of children to be born with missing or malformed limbs.[30] No limitations, regulations or framework for the human use of novel drugs had been in place up to that point. About a decade later, in the lab of Dr Judah Folkman, the discovery of the role of angiogenesis (the new formation of blood vessels) in certain diseases, such as leprosy, HIV and cancer, brought interest back to THAL.[31] Furthermore, in the early 1990s, research pioneers Dr Gilla Kaplan and Dr Bart Barlogie hypothesized that a rare blood cancer – also highly vascularized and referred to as multiple myeloma (MM) – may be treated with THAL.[29]

And it was. Here is how.

About the time of Dr Kaplan and Dr Barlogie's observations, I had started my medical residency. I recall treating MM patients and breaking the bad news to them of a relatively short average life expectancy of two to three years. There was little we could do to ease their suffering, which included anemia, bone pain and debilitating immune insufficiency. Basically, no therapy would be able to change that natural course.

Fast-forward three decades to the mid-2000s, I had joined Celgene Corporation, the company that had purchased and received FDA approval to manufacture THAL in 1995. By 1999, the pivotal clinical trial in refractory MM patients had demonstrated significant clinical benefits; the first improvement in over thirty years.[32] Together with ASCT (autologous stem cell transplantation), this now substantially improves patients' outcomes compared with my early training days as a resident.[33]

The incredible consequence of this discovery, though, was the exponential growth of the interest of pharmaceutical companies and academic research labs in what is actually considered a relatively 'rare' disease. Celgene alone developed two subsequent next-generation products, lenalidomide and pomalidomide, and you can search any larger pharma company's portfolio to find several products in development for treating MM patients.

In 2020, thanks to a virtuous circle of investments, discoveries and new treatments, and a fruitful level of cooperation between academia and industry, MM patients live about twice as long as they did when I started my medical residency thirty years ago: between seven to ten years.[18]

THE VICIOUS CIRCLE

Now, let's look behind the curtains of cost and affordability.

There is no doubt that we are having an issue of affordability in health care. The system is plagued by inefficiencies and waste. No other industry would have persisted so long, and accepted the small margins of profitability and inefficient use of resources, as we do in health care. An OECD analysis in 2017 summarized the main drivers for waste in health care in three parts: clinical (overtesting, errors, avoidable adverse effects), operational (overtreating, overprescribing, inefficient resource utilization) and system waste (administration, fraud and corruption).[34,35] Dr Marty Makary, in his latest bestselling book, *The Price We Pay*, describes these types of waste as root causes of our ailing health care systems and of the public's eroding trust in such systems.[36] What he describes for the US has been observed and documented in many other places.[2,10]

However, it is not as easy as blaming "bad pharma" or "stingy payers" or "greedy doctors." If it was that easy, we would have fixed the problems in health care a long time ago. In an era of constant information overload, it has become a challenge to filter out the inflating amount of fake news coming at us through multiple channels. Hence, it is more important than ever to get the facts straight in order to be able to provide a meaningful contribution to the health care debate.

I asked earlier: where does all the money go? Although the current fragmentation in an FFS system does not allow us to measure a full cycle of care per patient, there is enough evidence to grasp the big-picture spending. Ultimately, reducing drug prices will not reverse the trend of shortening life expectancy, or the wasteful nature of care delivery.

Here is why.

The cost of prescription drugs is an important part of the equation, but the crux of the discussion is to realize that it's not the only part of the overall health care expenditure pie. A pie that equals billions to trillions per year, as discussed earlier.

We do not have a problem of resource shortages in health care. We have an issue of resources in the wrong place.

Let's have a look at some of the facts.

Figure 1.7. The top three cost drivers in a country's health care expenditure.

	Total Budget 100%		**Waste** 20–50%	**Hospital** >30%	**Drugs** 10–20%
United States (USD)	$4,000 billion		$800-2,000 billion	> $1,000 billion	17% ($680 billion)
Switzerland (CHF)	CHF 80 billion		CHF 16-40 billion	> CHF 25 billion	7% (CHF 5.6 billion)
Germany (EUR)	€376 billion		€75-188 billion	> €100 billion	14% (€53 billion)

Sources [2, 10, 37-41]

1. Prescription drugs make up about ten percent, in some countries up to twenty percent, of the overall spend on health care. Figure 1.7 provides detailed examples of some countries. What these examples show is that at least eighty percent

of a national budget is actually spent on things *other* than prescription drugs.

So, what are these other big drivers of health care expenditure?

2. As depicted in the middle of figure 1.7, the single most costly factor is the hospital sector, which is accountable for more than thirty per cent of health care expenditure. I discovered that this number was not only consistent over time, but also consistent across geographies. Somehow, this is not astonishing. In general, the growth of the provider sector evolved in parallel to the progress in medicine over the past 100 years. However, on the flip side, hospitals will likely undergo the most fundamental transformation – and condensation away from chronic into acute, episodic and hyperspecialized care – over the next decade. In the following chapters, I will explore in more detail how the provider sector is affected most by the current imbalance of innovation and affordability and what the future of digital holds for its renewal in chapter four.

Lastly, no debate on affordability is complete without talking about waste.

3. Waste is the big elephant in the room, which is the reason why most proponents shy away from addressing it. It is so much easier to single out one drug cost than a myriad of reasons for wasteful care delivery, inefficient supply chains and excessive hospital costs. However, we cannot successfully renew and transform our health care systems without getting the facts right. I have been shocked to learn that twenty to fifty percent of health care delivery is considered wasteful,

and, again, this is consistent over time and geographies. Running the math, and taking the conservative end of the range, in the examples of the US and Switzerland this could mean up to one trillion US dollars and thirty billion Swiss francs of wasted money. How many problems could we solve with that much money?

Figure 1.8. The elephant in the room: waste in health care.

Having spent many years as an internist and oncologist in the hospital setting, I have witnessed many times the idiosyncrasies of what an inefficient health care delivery model looks like. However, during the research phase for this book, what astonished me most was the extent of quantifiable inefficiencies and the openness of doctors in speaking about it. First put in motion by Dr Marty Makary's book, *Unaccountable*, the taboo of doctors talking about their own practices further evolved in Thomas Koulopoulos' book *Reimagining Healthcare*.[36,42] In it, he describes survey results in which physicians self-reported an unnecessary amount of testing and treating (as high as twenty to twenty-five percent). The reasons for this "defensive medicine" are many, but one can imagine that fear of malpractice, type of education, and an overall culture of "doing" and "producing" are part of it.

Too much testing, too much treating, and too little scrutiny of what's really needed to drive better outcomes for patients are the true underlying issues.

Essentially, these numbers reflect what many refer to as a "crashed fee-for-service system", leading to inefficiencies, a fragmented value chain, and a set of solo dancers running the show of health care.

REBALANCING THE SYSTEM

Maintaining innovation, and finding more cures for cancer and other life-threatening diseases, is reaching a dead-end. Everyone wants precision medicine and better health outcomes. But waiting for a miracle and for "someone else" to find the magic bullet is fruitless.

Transformation in health care starts with awareness.

We need to shape the future of health care together. And we literally have no time to waste.

Understanding the underlying root causes of our broken health care systems requires a closer look behind the curtain and under the spotlight on drug costs. Realizing that it is not the pharmaceutical industry, not the payers, and not the providers alone that account for the imbalance is step number one. Step number two then allows us to explore the factors that contribute to the affordability issue in a more holistic way. Every link in the chain of health care is interconnected.

This will require a fundamental mindset shift from quantity to quality, from volume to value, and from a solo-dancing competition to cooperation within a *Tango for Five* (figure 1.9). We'll explore this in more detail in chapter two.

Figure 1.9. A fundamental mindset shift to drive health care transformation.

FROM	TO
Fix	Prevent
Reactive	Proactive
Solo	Together
More	Less
Volume	Value
Short term	Long term
Illness	**Health**

TOP TAKEAWAYS FROM CHAPTER ONE

☑ We are facing an imbalance between innovation and afford-ability in health care. Many decades of fruitful research and collaboration between academia and industry have resulted in massive longevity gains. However, as resources are limited, affordability is now a bottleneck.

☑ It is paramount to realize that our underlying issue is not a lack of resources in health care, but an overwhelming degree of waste and inefficiencies. This is a man-made problem. So, the solution lies with us, with everyone.

☑ Change starts with awareness. We can see that the problem and the solution do not lie with one actor only. The complexity and interconnectivity of the health care sector require a holistic approach. If all five actors rally behind a common purpose, we will be able to address the imbalance between innovation and affordability. This is the focus of the next chapter.

CHAPTER 2

Strengthening the interconnectivity of the top five actors in health care

*"We cannot solve the problems with the same
thinking we used when we created them."*

~ ALBERT EINSTEIN

MORE IS NOT ALWAYS BETTER

In 1984, Freddie Mercury was singing *"I Want To Break Free"*. It was one of the many megahits of the rock band Queen. At this time, Freddie could not guess just how real this shout-out would become for him personally. Just one year before, researchers had discovered the human immunodeficiency virus, better known as HIV, which would soon lead to a modern health epidemic. Freddie Mercury would succumb to this new disease, AIDS, in 1991.

In 1992, I arrived in Lausanne for my fourth year of medical school. I had signed up for my first in-patient rotation in the department of infectious diseases. At the time, a team of world-renowned researchers from clinics and pharmaceutical companies was collaborating to find novel treatments to help patients infected by HIV, who were dying from opportunistic infections and cancer because of their failing immune system. This was the start of a fruitful public-private partnership between pharma, academic institutions and patients. They were collaborating in search of a vaccine and an effective treatment to help patients suffering from HIV-AIDS. Although we still don't have a vaccine, the progress in terms of treatment has been revolutionary. Today, patients can attain an almost normal life expectancy thanks to an approved "tritherapy", which has been developed in close collaboration between pharma and academia. Furthermore, broad educational campaigns, supported by celebrities around the world, contributed to public awareness and reduced the spread and contagion of the disease.[43,44]

In hindsight, I did not realize that I was part of a unique experience: the first successful cooperation between an emerging pharmaceutical industry and academia.

Also, as I only appreciated much later, it was really the first time that the role of empowered patients taking ownership of their illness came into the limelight. Addressing wellbeing from a holistic perspective, where pills and treatments are only part of the equation, meant elements such as self-determined living and ownership of their condition rose to equal importance. (This was accelerated by the simultaneous rise of the internet and the real-time availability of information to patients and doctors.)

Fast-forward one decade to 1999, when, as a young resident in oncology, I witnessed a wave of enthusiasm for so-called high-dose chemotherapy and transplant (ASCT). This meant that the dosing of cytotoxic chemotherapy could be increased to a point that it would be lethal, but the patient could be saved by the infusion of their own stem cells. This would enable them to reconstitute their immune system after the chemo wiped out the cancer. Within a decade of being developed, this strategy was successfully curing children and adults from leukemia. The oncology community was led to believe that this strategy would work just as well for solid tumors such as breast cancer. However, the day I presented a clinical study to test such a strategy to a thirty-nine-year-old breast cancer patient in my outpatient clinic, the doubt behind using high-dose chemo for solid tumors had already started spreading. Also, to my great surprise, the patient eventually rejected my proposal to do this study.

Long story short; in general, patients follow their doctor's advice. In the case of a deadly disease, such as advanced cancer, a minority of patients would reject the proposal of participating in a clinical study that may lead to a better, albeit experimental, treatment. So, this patient taught me a great lesson in humility. Why? A week after our initial conversation, she returned to my clinic to tell me that she initially was favorable on thinking about it, but then eventually didn't want to take part in the study anyways. On seeing my surprised look, she offered me the following feedback: *"When we first spoke, YOU did not sound convinced yourself. You know, I have small children and I want to be in the best condition I possibly can be in order to spend as much quality time as I can with them. Your proposal – of weeks and months in isolation, feeling sick and unwell for the uncertain prospect of living a few months longer – isn't worth trying it. Sorry to disappoint you."*

Following the early rumors, the doubts were confirmed a couple of years later when we learned that the higher dose of chemo did not add that supposed survival benefit for breast cancer patients. But it certainly had added substantial toxicity, as my patient had feared.

Known as one of the big scandals in clinical research, this so-called "Bezwoda-case" (after the name of the lead investigator) had been a tragedy with all of the study data being falsified. After the initial 'hype,' we had to conclude that there was no benefit for high-dose chemo in breast cancer after all.[45-47] In addition to the personal lesson in humility, this episode was a lesson for us collectively in the researcher community: one of humility, of the risk of bias, and of the importance of evidence-based medicine and research rigor.

So, overall, my patient had intuitively made the right choice for her.

In addition to the notion that more is not always better, this episode also reminds us that solo dancers in medical research are rarely successful and that good things take teamwork and time.

Fast-forward another fifteen years to 2014, when I was once again part of a dramatic breast cancer story. One of my team members was twenty-six years old and breastfeeding her first child when she was diagnosed with metastatic disease to the bone and liver. A devastating diagnosis. Less than fifty percent of women in this advanced stage of disease live more than five years. Now, almost seven years later, she is still enjoying her first remission of disease, solely based on novel treatments such as monoclonal antibodies that are specifically designed and targeted to eradicate breast cancer cells. Although not a cure per se, this long-term treatment allows patients to live without visible cancer and with optimal quality of life, similar to the HIV situation. My first breast cancer patient in the 1990s did not have these options because these molecular make-ups on breast cancer cells hadn't been discovered yet, and the pharmaceutical industry hadn't developed the tailored remedies, such as these monoclonal antibodies.

Remember, more is not always better. Here is a quick overview of the points discussed so far:

- Urgency forges public-private coalitions, as showcased by the HIV-AIDS epidemic in the 1980s, when patients, physicians, pharma and policy rallied to contain and effectively treat the disease. We are experiencing this phenomenon again as I am writing this book with the COVID-19 pandemic.
- Patient empowerment and self-determined decision-making are critical to effective care delivery, in addition to a transparent doctor-patient relationship rooted in trust. Patients read doctors' body language and exactly know how to take the doctor's choice of words.
- Thoughtful innovation and rigor in clinical research can spare resources and toxicities and, overall, allow patients to maintain a longer lifespan and better quality of life.

LESS IS MORE

As we explored in chapter one, the path to the Holy Grail in health care is through the reduction of waste. We need to focus on less, but on the right things, and do it together.

An essential component adding fuel to the fire is the dysconnectivity between the main actors. Historically, health care has been operating as a disconnected group of silos. Everyone looks at their own territory: pharma within pharma, providers within providers, payers within payers, policy within policy. We rarely look left or right to see who depends on our decisions and who could impact ours. We rarely look before or after to see what happens to patients in their home environments and what the results of our treatments are. Additionally, the culture has been largely hierarchical, paternalistic and slow in adopting change. Consequently, the health care industry as a whole has remained vastly stagnant over the past century. It somehow missed the train to customer-centricity and the Fourth Industrial Revolution, both of which have led to fundamental transformation in other industries. Medical education and the overall FFS system have focused on testing, treating and generally doing as much as possible. Conversely, the expectation from society, and patients more specifically, has been to receive a pill for everything (figure 1.1) – so much so that only doctors who "do something" are considered good doctors.

We need to break down silos and the perception that action equals quality.

This silo-like mentality constantly leads to missed opportunities. That is, chances to make a real impact on patients' lives. If only we would take into consideration what is important to them, and with whom we need to partner in order to address those needs. Instead of asking why a test needs to be done or a treatment needs to be delivered, we need to ask: what problem are we aiming to solve and how can we solve it together?

Our health care systems are at breaking point. This is not a controversial statement.

What *is* more controversial is the notion that we are in this together, sharing responsibility.

Yes, there is an affordability issue in health care, as we have seen in the previous chapter.

But in addition to cost, waste and quality, we have an issue of trust that underpins the silo-like mentality.

Patients not trusting doctors, insurers and pharma. Pharma not trusting policymakers and payers. Payers not trusting pharma or policy. Overall distrust seems to be at an all-time high, which in turn further deepens divides, partisan perceptions and transactional ways of working. In this environment, we have tunnel vision and are quick to lament who the putative (other) villain is. As human nature goes, we rarely find that villain in our own peer group. We need to stop the narrative of blame and guilt. If finger-pointing in health care were justified, wouldn't we have fixed our problems? In contrast, the complexity in health care requires complex solutions. And everyone needs to contribute.

For leaders in health care, solving problems starts with acknowledging that in this hypercomplex ecosystem, each and every actor is highly interdependent along the entire value chain: patients receiving care, doctors delivering care, pharmaceuticals developing care, payers paying for care, and policymakers safeguarding the ethics and regulations for all these tight interactions. This system simply doesn't work if you only look at one piece at a time. Furthermore, the complexity in health care is so vast – and the sets of expertise so diverse – that differing cultures, jargon and concerns in each group are hard to bridge. However, given the tight interdependency, the solutions to each group's problems often lie with another group and set of expertise. We will discuss some of these intricacies in much more detail later in this chapter, as well as in part two, when I elaborate on how value-based care principles, the digital revolution and a playbook for multi-party collaboration will catalyze joint problem-solving.

For now, it is all about connections and trying to solve the broken health care system together. No one can do it alone. In the following sections, we will review the individual sets of frustrations and interests of each of the five main actors in health care. Then, I will share examples of successful partnership models, which only work when silos are broken down and synergies are unfolded.

Once we collectively break down silos, reconnect the dots and forge novel partnerships, we will be able to identify synergies, eliminate waste, and restore the balance between innovation and affordability.

FRUSTRATION AND INTERESTS

The one element that seems to act as an equalizer among all actors is a widespread level of frustration with the overall situation. However, the reasons behind these frustrations, and the solutions to remediate them, couldn't be more different. Ultimately, though, it comes down to a lack of understanding of each group's situation, needs and pressures. Continued competition over resources and costs is only deepening the divides. Perhaps doctors have an appreciation of the difficulties that their patients face in navigating complexities and fighting financial constraints. Maybe patients can empathize with nurses and doctors when they see them struggling with overwhelming administrative burden. However, rarely is there an understanding as to why an insurer, a pharmaceutical company, a hospital administrator or a policymaker would have their own set of frustrations.

Having spent close to twenty years of my professional career in the provider sector, I feel very close to the unique situation of physicians and also patients. Further, after twelve years as a business leader in the pharmaceutical sector, I can also relate to the struggles and interests of those within the private life sciences sector, as well as payers and policymakers. Looking at this collective experience, and after speaking with many representatives in the ecosystem, it appears that progress will only be feasible through all participants acting with empathy, understanding mutual frustrations and clarifying everyone's interests.

The solutions to the quandary in health care are contingent on all actors within the public AND the private sectors contributing with their sets of expertise.

In the spirit of raising awareness, building bridges and identifying possibilities for new partnerships, the main objective of this chapter is to share examples of their respective 'day job' pressures: patients, providers, pharma, payers and policymakers. In doing so, I hope to highlight some of the most pressing underlying concerns, and any areas of common ground.

Here's a brief overview of the frustrations and interests of the five main actors.

Figure 2.1. The frustrations and interests of the five main actors in health care.

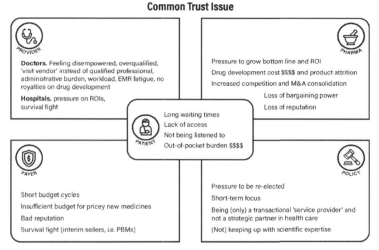

5P LEADERS' FRUSTRATIONS
Common Trust Issue

PROVIDER

Doctors. Feeling disempowered, overqualified, 'visit vendor' instead of qualified professional, administrative burden, workload, EMR fatigue, no royalties on drug development

Hospitals. pressure on ROIs, survival fight

PHARMA

Pressure to grow bottom line and ROI

Drug development cost $$$$ and product attrition

Increased competition and M&A consolidation

Loss of bargaining power

Loss of reputation

PATIENT

Long waiting times
Lack of access
Not being listened to
Out-of-pocket burden $$$$

PAYER

Short budget cycles

Insufficient budget for pricey new medicines

Bad reputation

Survival fight (interim sellers, i.e. PBMs)

POLICY

Pressure to be re-elected

Short-term focus

Being (only) a transactional 'service provider' and not a strategic partner in health care

(Not) keeping up with scientific expertise

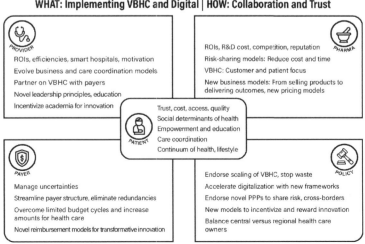

GOAL: RECONCILING 5P INTERESTS
WHAT: Implementing VBHC and Digital | HOW: Collaboration and Trust

PROVIDER

ROIs, efficiencies, smart hospitals, motivation

Evolve business and care coordination models

Partner on VBHC with payers

Novel leadership principles, education

Incentivize academia for innovation

PHARMA

ROIs, R&D cost, competition, reputation

Risk-sharing models: Reduce cost and time

VBHC: Customer and patient focus

New business models: From selling products to delivering outcomes, new pricing models

PATIENT

Trust, cost, access, quality
Social determinants of health
Empowerment and education
Care coordination
Continuum of health, lifestyle

PAYER

Manage uncertainties

Streamline payer structure, eliminate redundancies

Overcome limited budget cycles and increase amounts for health care

Novel reimbursement models for transformative innovation

POLICY

Endorse scaling of VBHC, stop waste

Accelerate digitalization with new frameworks

Endorse novel PPPs to share risk, cross-borders

New models to incentivize and reward innovation

Balance central versus regional health care owners

Let's now look at each group in more detail.

THE PATIENT

In the digital twenty-first century, where information is only a fingertip away, the patient's power as "consumer" holds more weight than ever before.

———————————

Patients are expecting health care "on demand" and want a trustworthy and empathetic provider-doctor relationship in which doctors listen to their needs and tailor care accordingly.

———————————

Traditional health care delivery is being disrupted by "Dr Google", as well as patient influencers on social media who take on prominent roles in terms of promoting or condemning various treatment choices and overall aspects around quality of life. Empowered patients are often seeking more holistic recommendations, including emotional, societal, work-related and spiritual components. As such, the patient experience and journey along the health continuum – from prevention to long-term care – is coming into focus, as I discuss in more detail in chapter three.

Renate Brentjes, a patient who took on a leadership role as CEO of the Advisory Council on Care for the Dutch Ministry of Health, takes it one step further. *"You are there for me; I am there for you."* What she refers to is her own view of an empowered patient: considering it as a chance *and* duty to be a pro-active partner for innovation and clinical research.[48]

However, today's reality is still largely different in many places, although it has to be acknowledged that things are changing, as Renate indicates. What many patients are still facing today is a patronizing culture, long waiting times, limited access to care, and financial toxicity in terms of premiums and out-of-pocket expenses. They feel disconnected from the value chain and are often the ones losing out most in a dysfunctional health care system.

THE PROVIDER

The doctor-patient relationship is the backbone of health care. No doctor, no care. People choose to become a doctor because they want to help patients, are curious about science, and are passionate about medicine. Referred to as "Dr Burnout" or "visit vendors" in an FFS system, many though have become disillusioned.[49-51]

What doctors and nurses want is more time.
More quality time spent with the patient
and less time wasted with bureaucracy.

I have been shocked by recent statistics highlighting the extent of frustration with my own profession. Within oncology, one out of two health professionals suffer from severe burnout. In 2020, Dr Eric D Tetzlaff, a physician assistant at Fox Chase Cancer Center, published a survey study reporting that self-reported burnout in physician assistants increased from 34.8 per cent in 2015 to 48.7 per cent in 2019.[52] Severe emotional exhaustion, deper-sonalization and a low sense of accomplishment are only a few of the reported symptoms. The introduction of electronic medical records (EMRs) over the past decade has only worsened this situation for both doctors and nurses.[2,53,54] Built to make billing more efficient, but designed without any input from the end user, these first-generation EMRs missed the real purpose, which is to make the work of doctors and nurses more efficient. Instead, EMRs created a bottleneck, multiplied paperwork, worsened mistrust, and forged a disbelief that things will ever change for the better. As depicted in figure 2.2., breaking under the burden to produce and the pressure to meet relative value unit (RVU) numbers, a colleague recently summarized the situation to me as follows: *"If you add one more useless initiative and one more piece of paperwork, I'll jump out the window."*[55,56]

Figure 2.2. Pointless administrative burdens and bureaucracy.

To complicate things further, there is a co-dependency between health care workers and their respective administrators. The majority of care in today's system is delivered within the hospital setting, as highlighted in chapter one, with hospitals being the single largest (growing) contributor to the spending mix, so much so that profitability, margins and ROIs are getting skewed year after year. Today, hospitals have become a source of major inefficiencies because of outdated infrastructures, analog processes and transactional ways of working, producing an excessive volume of visits and quantity of procedures. However, at the same time, this sector is undergoing a massive transformation, with the nature of care delivery changing to a home-based focus, and self-empowered patients claiming more transparency and digitalization, and the smart revolution pushing hard on digital in hospitals.

Digitalization, the power of the consumer-patient, and outcomes-based principles are at our doorstep and will define the smart hospitals of the future.

As discussed in an informative panel discussion on the *Future of Hospitals* at the World Economic Forum (WEF) in Davos, Switzerland in 2019, the provider networks most willing to adapt to change and take on an outcomes-based, patient-centric strategy, will prevail.[57] During the discussion, Dr Stephen Klasko, CEO at Jefferson Health, summarized it perfectly: *"In the future, we will be measured based on how healthy our population is and not how many patients fill in our beds."*[58] Along the same lines, and as I describe in more detail in chapters three and four, a number of large hospitals are putting forward multi-year strategies to fundamentally transform their infrastructure, processes and reward systems. This includes examples such as the Essen University Hospital in Germany and the Oak Street Health consortium in the US.[87,134]

PHARMA

One of the peculiarities in the health care industry has been that research and development (R&D) of new drugs has been almost monopolized within the private sector. Recently, the pharmaceutical industry has grown into a broader, vibrant life science sector spanning from traditional pharma companies to "Med Tech" and digital health enterprises. As a reminder from chapter one, given the high failure rate and long development timelines, R&D is a high-cost, high-risk endeavor. Therefore, up to now, only large, private companies were able to propel the level of innovation we have seen. Make no mistake; this model has brought unprecedented advances in medicine for over half a century. But it has also marginalized the contribution of the public academic sector in terms of monetary rewards. Clinical trials cannot be done without patients, or without physicians. However, neither one "belongs" under the authority of pharmaceutical companies. Nevertheless, the academic contribution to this partnership has produced innumerable successes in terms of scientific discoveries and therapeutic advances (see the thalidomide breakout box in the previous chapter). However, what is rarely talked about is that academic institutions, researchers and doctors are not part of the ROIs and do not get royalties from these product developments or commercialization successes. People are asking: why is only pharma reaping the benefits when doctors and patients are a key part of the innovative development?

Overall, this monopoly exacerbates the silo mentality and bargaining power, both of which prevent collaborative partnerships to collectively address the problems in health care. Moving forward, we need to reflect on how to broaden this monopoly, asking: how can we innovate innovation in medicine?

What we need is a public-private dialogue around how we can further evolve the monopoly of drug development into broader incentives for the public and the private sector alike.

"What do you mean, 'frustration in pharma'?" This is usually the reaction during dinner table discussions when I start talking about the topic. "They are making tons of money. Why would they be frustrated?" Yes, this is one perspective. There is no doubt that there must be reform on how to structure payment and reimbursement models around value generators, and these need to be elaborated on together with payers, policymakers and patients. Another perspective, though, is that pharma is under pressure with regard to profitability and ROIs because of increasing competition and development costs. The R&D cost is weighing heavily on the balance of affordability and not all parties perceive the returning benefits as equitable. As a consequence, pharma is often considered the villain in the public debate. Rarely does it hit headlines for its groundbreaking contribution to innovation and the fact that this innovation is saving many lives.

In an increasingly value-based world, new products have to show breakthrough potential to transform the natural course of a disease and to solve an unmet need in order to justify R&D and commercialization cost.

Priorities are shifting radically. As Marco Bertini and Oded Koenigsberg describe in their book, *The Ends Game*, industries must shift from selling products to delivering outcomes if they want to survive an increasingly fierce competition for resources.[59] They argue that it is a generalizable concept in the twenty-first century that customers choose products and services that deliver the best end results, the best experience and the best value to them. Something like a "Netflix for all". Health care is no different. Pharma is no different. The traditional pharmaceutical market is already being disrupted by agile start-up companies that do not carry legacy infrastructure, processes and assets, and therefore are more likely to adapt and adopt the tools of the Fourth Industrial Revolution more efficiently, as we shall see in chapter four.[60,61]

THE PAYER

Different countries have different archetypes for health payment structures. In some countries, paying for health is under the public authority, with drug pricing and reimbursement underlying national, regional and local formularies. In the US, health care is largely private, with insurers, health systems and plans following different mechanisms. For the interested reader, I refer you to Dr Zeke Emanuel's comprehensive overview, *Which Country Has the World's Best Health Care?*, which describes in much detail up-to-date information on payer, provider and policy structures in eleven countries.[2] For the purpose of this book, I am focusing on the fact that care has to be funded somehow, and that there are commonalities in needs and pressures among all payer structures.

Generally speaking, in health care, payers are an intermediary between the buyer and the manufacturer. There is no direct-to-consumer financial flow in the traditional health care FFS model.

Experts from the private and public sectors need to find a way to transform our outdated payment and reimbursement models in health care.

Additionally, budget cycles for health care payers are usually disproportionally shorter than the benefit of services and products they provide. What unites all systems is that a lack of transparency in the supply chain of products and services introduces high degrees of uncertainties to manage that budget. What does that mean? Payer systems have been set up typically to pay for a one-time service, such as a pill to remediate headache or surgery to fix a broken leg, so costs are well understood. In the case of chronic treatments for conditions like diabetes or heart failure, costs can also be relatively well managed because the number of patients affected, the duration, and the dosing of the therapy are predictable.

However, in the case of breakthrough and transformative therapies – which have the potential to cure patients and save lives – this calculation doesn't work quite the same way. In 2017, curative cell and gene therapies for cancer – such as the novel CAR T-cell therapies – cost the payer up to half a million US dollars.[62,63] In 2019, the gene therapy Zolgensma, which cures young children with fatal muscular atrophy, cost the payer and the patient $2 million.[64,65] This sounds prohibitive. However, since the underlying natural course of the disease is radically changed, the real underlying question now is: how much is a life worth?

This requires a societal, political and
health professional debate to determine
how a society sets priorities.

Singling out villains won't fix the problem and shooting the messenger is likely to kill further innovation. If we want to maintain the pace of transformational innovation, we need a fundamental reset regarding the way we reimburse and value therapies instead.

THE POLICYMAKER

Health care doesn't operate in a vacuum. It is one of the most regulated industries. For good reason, too. The overall goal must always be to safeguard ethical standards, and people's integrity and safety. As outlined in chapter one (in breakout box 1), the thalidomide disaster led to the Declaration of Helsinki by the World Medical Association (WMA) in 1964, now clearly outlining the ethical principles and standards for medical research involving human beings.[66] Subsequently, regulatory health authorities as we know them today were introduced, scrutinizing the benefit-risk ratio for each new product, device or solution that is deemed to intervene with an individual's life. Hurdles and stakes are high, and the process to meet these regulatory requirements is complex, expensive and risky.

However, over time, in a well-intentioned attempt to fix the fragmentation in health care, a patchwork mentality and an increasing number of new policies inadvertently only added further complexity to the system. This is because these policies were created in isolation and without the required consideration of the interconnectivity of the root causes.

The challenge for policy is that most players in this sector are elected officials. The sector comprises politicians, lawmakers and professionals appointed by politicians, such as the heads of health agencies (for example, the FDA commissioner in the US, who is appointed by the country president). The risk of implementing disruptive new regulations comes with the risk of not being re-elected. This quandary in and of itself is fueling risk-adversity and change resistance, which can only be overcome by a multi-pronged, multi-partner effort.

When it comes to policy and regulators, what we need is creativity and innovation instead of transactional service provider relationships between the public and private sectors.

Historically, there has been a deep mistrust between the public not-for-profit and the private for-profit sectors. In order to make progress, we need to break down these perceived barriers and avoid reinventing the wheel. In traditional silo-mentality settings, the tendency is for pharma, providers and payers to look at regulatory agencies as a kind of service provider to approve and reimburse drugs. What we need instead is a fundamental mindset shift to look at policy as a proactive and strategic partner. Particularly in light of the digital revolution pushing hard on health care, the opportunity here is unique. In order to keep up with innovation and the pace of digital transformation, we need a proactive and agile approach to policy, co-creating the required new regulatory frameworks together.

THE NORTH STAR:
PARTNERSHIPS ACROSS SECTORS

So, what does "good" look like? What does the future hold for health care?

What is certain is that we need to overcome statements such as: "Your company is run by lawyers! You are really hard to work with," as I heard too many times in my days in pharma. The path to sustainable health care means breaking down silos by removing regulatory, legal and economic barriers to foster collaboration. With a radical mindset shift (see figure 1.9), we can build bridges, strengthen the interconnectivity, and forge novel partnerships between patients, providers, pharma, payers and policy.

Here are a few examples of public-private partnerships (PPP) that highlight the feasibility of successfully juggling various sets of interests, both outside and within health care.

Project SpaceX

One example outside of health care is Elon Musk's space shuttle project, *SpaceX*.[67] As a private entrepreneur, Musk is hoping to provide commercial air travel into space and eventually travel to Mars by leveraging NASA's public sector expertise.[68-70] In the fall of 2020, the program pioneered the first manned flight, SpaceX Demo-2, launching two NASA astronauts into space. NASA selected

SpaceX to develop a lunar-optimized starship to transport crew between the lunar orbit and the surface of the Moon as part of NASA's Artemis program.[71]

Why does this work in a domain that you may judge non-essential, compared with a domain as essential as health care and protecting people's health? During the 2020 pandemic, people were wondering: "We are flying to Mars, but can't put in place digital contact tracing for people on earth?" Some people say it is because the private sector is in the driver's seat, while others argue it is because it is a non-essential area and therefore "no one cares." Isn't it what happens when you stop interfering and leave experts, visionaries and funding sources to do what they do best: be creative and innovate? A blueprint for health care? I believe it is.

The COVID-19 coalition

When the stakes are as high as they can get – a pandemic ravaging lives and livelihoods – the impossible becomes possible, even in health care. Case in point: COVID-19 and the subsequent race to develop a vaccine. In under one year, several vaccines have been produced by multiple actors, start-up companies, large pharmaceuticals, the FDA, the NIH and the WHO working together.[72] "Operation Warp Speed" bridged the FDA, the US Department of Health and Human Services and several pharma companies with military leadership in logistics and operations. The operation was co-led by a four-star general, scientists and regulators.[73] Furthermore, the ACTIV coalition (Accelerating COVID-19 Therapeutic Interventions and Vaccines), under the auspices of the NIH and the leadership of Dr Fauci and colleagues, regrouped US and European regulators as well as numerous pharma companies behind the same single objective of fighting this unprecedented public health crisis.[74]

Notice the difference? In the traditional innovation model, as we have known it in the past fifty years, all of the cost and risk is carried by one owner, one company. In the case of COVID-19, academia, industry and policymakers worked hand-in-glove in record-breaking time to study not only vaccines against the virus, but also possible therapeutics to treat it. A blueprint for future drug development and innovation in medicine? I believe it is.

The Pancreatic Cancer Platform

For a forty-year-old patient who is diagnosed with pancreatic cancer, life turns grim. The average life expectancy is less than one year, and treatment options are scarce and toxic. There has been no tangible progress and innovation in this field for over forty years, and it has not been for a lack of trying.[75] Multiple companies, researchers and funding sources have attempted to fight this deadly cancer, but only with limited success. In light of this, an unprecedented coalition of doctors, patients, pharma companies and policymakers created the Pancreatic Cancer European Multi-Stakeholder Platform.[76] With the aim of doubling survival rates in the decade to come, it approached the European Commission to prioritize this cancer in order to attack it from multiple angles: better education and earlier diagnosis by primary care physicians and also patients, better connection between basic and clinical research, and a more concerted effort between public and private to share risks and costs. A prime example for other coalitions to fight cancer and beyond? I believe it is.

The AMR action fund

Even though cancer is the second most common cause of death globally, death from multi-resistant bacteria is likely to eclipse cancer over the next two decades. In contrast to the oncology market, the antibiotics market has suffered from chronic de-investments and failures to innovate since I trained in the 1990s. One of the main reasons for this has been the challenge to produce sustainable ROIs. Business drives innovation, which drives longevity gains for people. In order to stimulate the fundamental renewal of R&D incentives to fight antimicrobial resistance (AMR), a public-private partnership has been created.[77] Over a dozen pharmaceutical companies, banks, foundations, associations and agencies have joined this fund, raising $1 billion to rapidly bring two to four novel antibiotics to the market. Although unknown to the broader public, could AMR become a PPP model for other therapeutic areas? I believe it could.

Collaborating is the new normal

If we don't cooperate, we won't make any progress to grow the collective value pie in health care.

Today, health care consists of asymmetrical relationships based on different purchasing power in an FFS system that eventually leads to destroying value. Tomorrow, what we need instead are mutual trusted partnerships that allow us to master complexity, cost and risks of innovation, and generate mutual-gain value together.

We can learn two things from the examples I've just shared.

Firstly, the potential of synergies is greatest when interrelationships span across multiple sectors, and whenever cost and risk are shared across various actors. Secondly, innovation flourishes at the intersection of these sectors, when subject matter experts have an opportunity to overlap and cross-fertilize. However, despite these encouraging partnerships happening in parts of the ecosystem, we have yet to fully realize the potential of interrelationships between industry, academia, payers, policymakers and patients.

What can we do to overcome these barriers and unleash a *Tango for Five* instead? And how can we perpetuate and scale what we have seen with these few examples?

Figure 2.3. Multi-party collaboration opportunities in the health care ecosystem.

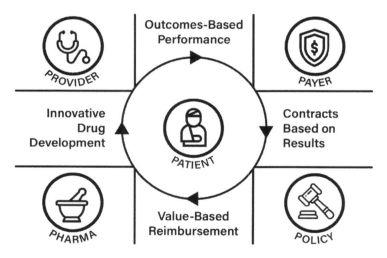

Figure 2.3 summarizes ideas and principles of multi-party synergies in health care. What is notable from this diagram is that the solution to each of the listed challenges requires the contribution of experts outside of each group. Let's have a look at each of these examples.

- Innovation and creativity for novel, more efficient and dig-italized clinical study designs for drug development occur between pharma, physicians in academia, patients and policymakers.
- Outcomes-based performance measurements to enhance value and efficiencies for providers demand alignment with payers, policymakers and patients.
- Multi-party agreements based on results-based rewards and incentives require contracts between payer, provider and pharma, and must be supported by policy.
- Novel pricing and reimbursement models for transformative new medicines not only require policy, payer, pharma and providers, but also societal debate and the input of patient views.

You don't need all five actors all the time. However, what becomes clear from these examples is that on the health care stage, it usually takes more than two to tango. In the grand scheme of things, however, and particularly from incremental to transformational impact, it requires all five.

What stands at the beginning of any scaling effort is the requirement to rebuild trust.

As you will see in the following chapter, focusing on the ultimate customer needs, which in health care are the patients' needs and outcomes, holds the power to naturally galvanize teamwork and restore trust among all actors.

TOP TAKEAWAYS FROM CHAPTER TWO

☑ Curiosity about each other's interests is the key to bringing novel partnerships to fruition. Changing our behavior from competing to cooperation, and deepening our interrelationships, will lead to overcoming fragmentation and the breaking down of silos.

☑ Recognizing that both innovation and efficiency gains happen at the intersections between the top five actors is what will drive the resolution of the quandary in health care.

☑ The next chapter outlines how this novel coordination across actors naturally moves the needle toward a balanced equation between innovation and affordability, so that we can ultimately generate value for all.

PART II

DO

CHAPTER 3

Applying value-based principles to redesign a patient-centered health system

"The whole is more than the sum of its parts."

~ ARISTOTLE

HOW FRAGMENTATION DESTROYS VALUE AND TRUST

When Hanna was ten years old, she was terrified of needles.

Just as any teen girl would be, or even any adult, at the idea of daily self-injections to stay alive. Hanna is one of over one million people under the age of twenty who live with type 1 diabetes. Overall, diabetes is one of the most prevalent diseases in the Western world, with a staggering 463 million people living with this chronic illness. That's one in ten adults aged twenty to seventy-nine years.[78]

Hanna wasn't allowed to share candy and sweets with her friends, and also had to be mindful of intensive sports. Frequent visits to the hospital ER were a common part of her life way into her adulthood. Because she struggled to balance nutrition, physical activity and treatments, she would often either be hypoglycemic (not enough blood sugar) or hyperglycemic (too much). Both of which came with severe episodes of fatigue upon recovery, keeping her away from school or the workplace for days and weeks.

Today, Hanna, an entrepreneur and patient expert, is very active in helping fellow patients to become proactive in managing their health, illness and life. I met Hanna during a panel discussion on collaboration in health care.[200] "*Where have you been all my life?*" we both said, always on the hunt for likeminded people. We, a patient and a doctor, reflected on how we can contribute to making health care a better and more connected place. That event triggered a series of common projects, including our joint article on the experience of the patient journey and the doctor-patient relationship.[79]

So, let's have a look at a few aspects of Hanna's story that beautifully exemplify the essentials of what we mean when we talk about value-based health care.

- "*I was ashamed of my own illness; I didn't want to handle it,*" she told me. People's self-esteem – children's and adults' alike – suffers when they are tagged "different" and excluded from everyday leisure and workplace activities. Just like many actors in the health care ecosystem, it is about managing that constant tension between short-term incentives and long-term consequences. For the patient, it means feeling good in the moment versus investing in your future life. **Understanding patients' needs and feelings is the first step to creating value.**

- *"I've not always been that self-educated patient I am today, but was rather 'an enfant terrible' during my teen years,"* says Hanna as she reflects on her thirty-five-year "career", as she puts it. It would take one last emergency landing in the ER, at age twenty-eight, for her to think, *"Soon I'll be dead if nothing changes."* She spent a considerable amount of time reflecting on what it means to her to become an empowered patient, which occurred *"only once I took my life into my own hands and figured out other ways to make me feel better, such as nutrition, sports, hydration and stress management, that suited my lifestyle and my illness."* **Self-empowered patients, and choosing options "beyond the pill" are an untapped potential on the way to value.**

- *"All these roller-coaster years with yo-yo blood sugars left me exhausted,"* she recounts, as she reflects on her struggles to navigate the indiscernible web of doctors, nurses, specialists, hospitals and community stations. A fragmented system and a silo mentality weighed heavily on her trust in doctors and nurses. *"However, the ones who struck me as my bright stars all had one very simple commonality: they listened to me. They were empathetic and took me, my concerns and my goals seriously and did not only see me as 'diabetes' but as a young woman with my own rights."* **Better care coordination and empathetic providers, who co-create treatment goals together with the patient, are the backbone of value creation.**

- What touched me most listening to Hanna was a deep feeling of loneliness that resulted from her various calamities. Not only concerns about her body, but also worries about her state of mind, which is part of a holistic cycle of care. *"Nobody spoke to me about mental health ever before,"* she concluded after her life-changing last visit to the ER. *"But I am so thrilled to see that there are solutions out there to help me and others!"* Today, several decades later and still living with diabetes, Hanna has made peace with her own struggles and feels supported by her care team. Notably, it was a patient nurse who didn't *"scoff over my fear of needles, but actually made a plan to work on helping me to overcome that fear and finally self-inject the insulin that I am so vitally dependent on."* **A holistic approach to health along the health continuum, from prevention to acute and chronic care, is what VBHC is all about.**

I have been asking myself: "Can't we do better?" Even in the best health care systems in the world, and despite having the best trained doctors and best innovative treatments, a young patient living with diabetes is still left in such despair that she actually thinks she may die before the age of thirty.

PATIENT CENTRICITY IS THE TOLLGATE TO VALUE

This is where value starts – with addressing people's personal needs. Not only in health care, but universally in any part of our lives. Asking, and listening to, what value means to the customer is the essential starting point in any industry. It is about personal choices that people want to make for themselves and the experience they envision when buying a product or a service.

> *"People don't want to buy a drill. People*
> *want to buy a hole in the wall."*
> ~THEODORE LEVITT

It is all about the job that needs to get done. Not the tool. This is what Professor Levitt at Harvard Business School was alluding to fifty years ago when he said that the customer's need and primary interest is the hole in the wall, not the drill.[80] To this day, it illustrates perfectly what we mean by customer-centricity. Consumers aren't interested in the tool they buy, but in the results they get from using it and the value that the outcomes represent for them. People go the movies not because they can't see the film at home, but because of the experience – and the ability to share that experience with others. People go to a restaurant not necessarily because they need food, but because they long for the experience of sharing and celebrating the occasion with others. Much of that feeling of experience is about connections with others.

In health care, however, the concept of customer-centricity and the importance of the consumer experience have been late to the show. In our context, the customer is the patient.

There is much that health care can learn from other industries when it comes to value, the customer experience, and learning how to listen to the consumer. This concept has been widely explored in various sectors, leading to successful renewals in the travel, hospitality, retail and tech industries. As Bertini and Koenigsberg state, *"smart companies stop selling products and start delivering value."*[59] In the twenty-first century, the new competitive edge in any industry lies in the ability to stop selling the "means" to an end (products, services and procedures) and to start delivering the "ends" to customers (results and outcomes that matter to consumers), they conclude. In their review of recent business successes, they demonstrate that this sequence of thinking and strategizing – consumer first, solutions second – actually generates value for all actors in any given industry. So, no different in health care.

Figure 3.1. Customer focus is the starting point to value generation.

However, isn't it ironic that we have to refer to the consumer goods and business world to help us refocus on who our ultimate customer is in health care – the patient? I have always found this astonishing. In fact, it leaves me with a bit of an odd aftertaste when considering: how can we eventually reconcile business interests, profitability and value generation in an industry where health is not a commodity? How come we as an industry have so terribly lost focus on the patient? How is it that we now need to make a concerted effort to create meaningful conversations with the patient? As we have seen in previous chapters, the frustration about this quandary is shared across the ecosystem, and we've gained an understanding of what created this dilemma.

Let's now look at how we can insert value-based principles into the health care ecosystem.

Delivering value to patients is the number one goal in health care.

What does value actually mean to patients?

Well, we have seen it in Hanna's story. Tailoring the treatment and a care plan so that it makes sense to her and involves her as an equal partner. Achieving the results that make her feel better today and preventing complications in the future. Working in a team that helps her live a healthier life personally and professionally, despite an underlying chronic illness.

Value to patients is all about the end-to-end experience.

It is about the patient journey and about what happens *before* and *after*. What happens at home? What happens on the way to the hospital or a doctor's appointment? What happens during a conversation with a nurse, during treatment, during surgery? What benefit does the patient derive from that new pill they're taking in the morning? Are they feeling better? Or does the patient stop the new treatment because it makes them feel dizzy? To highlight the crucial aspect of the end-to-end experience, I recall a recent conversation I had with my friend, asking for news about her father, who is what we would call a cancer survivor, having successfully battled colon cancer years ago. Although he is now free from cancer, my friend tells me, *"Verena, his quality of life is really miserable because of permanent incontinence. He has completely stopped going outdoors for a walk or joining us at restaurants. He has become so lonely."* His reduced mobility not only negatively impacts his wellbeing and social connections but, lately, also his trust in health care. This story exemplifies the importance of quality of life to patients and reminds us as doctors, drug developers and manufacturers to not focus solely on survival rates. Delivering value to patients means delivering optimal outcomes for them to enjoy both quality *and* quantity of life.

Improving outcomes for patients means that the patient must be part of the solution. Only once we truly understand what matters to patients will we be able to tailor care to their personal needs and co-create the right care plans.

The future of health care will lie with those who compete, cooperate and win on value. Value delivered to the customer. Other industries have long understood this concept of consumer focus, societal determinants and avoiding waste as an enabler for value. It is time that health care catches that train. There is no reason for it not to. There really is no other good alternative, either. Spinning the logic of customer-centricity beyond the patient and provider environment, value-based principles are taking root across the entire ecosystem. These include value-based pricing, value-based reimbursement and value-based procurement, to cite only a few (I also refer you back to figure 2.3). There is no shortage of literature and case studies available in the realm of both public health and the private life sciences sector.[81-83] There is no limit to the imagination when it comes to patient-centered value strategies, which are good for patients and the businesses in health care alike.

"If the health care industry were to fully embrace a continuous customer-only, demand-side approach, it could literally transform health care delivery and health outcomes," summarizes Dr Zeev Neuwirth in his landmark book, *Reframing Healthcare.* The book outlines how health care leaders can become disruptors that move the needle toward better systems of health. It was a great source of inspiration for me to write *It Takes Five to Tango.*[3]

Putting the focus right back onto the ultimate customer, the patient, is intuitively the right thing to do in an industry that builds its whole reason for being around the health and wellbeing of people.

But, as we shall see, it is also the right thing to do to unlock the deep value generation for all other related stakeholders in the ecosystem: providers, payers, pharma and policymakers.

So, you may be thinking, "That sounds all good and obvious. But how do we get there? How can we possibly abandon a billing culture based on a fee-for-service model and replace it with something else?"

VBHC: THIS WON'T WORK!

Many of you living and working in the daily realities of hospitals, pharma, payers and policy may say, "This is a nice, rosy picture. It sounds great, but, in my reality, this will never work!" The problem is so big, the obstacles seem so high, and the complexity looks so vast, that indeed it may feel overwhelming and intimidating to believe that change is even feasible. Powerplays and positional bargaining have brought us to a place where we do not believe that change is even possible. As we have seen in chapter two, the frustrations have grown so big that they make us sick – physically, emotionally and intellectually.

The good news is that change is indeed possible. By swapping our incentive systems from *rules on volume* to *principles of value*, it can be done. The initial trick to that transformation is to fundamentally change the narrative and start with the ingoing question: how can I drive quality up and improve outcomes that matter to patients? As we shall see from examples throughout this chapter, by making this question our new square one starting point, equitable value for all actors can be achieved.

_____

Finding the right treatment for the right patient at the right time is the essence of value-based health care.

_____

VBHC was first introduced to a broader health care audience by Michael Porter in 2006, and further refined in subsequent publications, presentations and real-life projects across the world.[84,85] Drawing on his earlier focus on business strategy in general, he writes, "*Business is caught in a vicious circle. A big part of the problem lies with companies themselves, which remain trapped in an outdated, narrow approach to value creation. Focused on optimizing short-term financial performance, they overlook the greatest unmet needs in the market as well as broader influences on their long-term success. Why else would companies ignore the wellbeing of their customers, the depletion of natural resources vital to their businesses, the viability of suppliers, and the economic distress of the communities in which they produce and sell?"*[86]

Translating these principles to health care, he established the now commonly accepted formula of VBHC: focusing on patient health outcomes and what is important in people's lives at efficient cost. This will ultimately generate real value. Not only to patients, but to all actors in the ecosystem. It allows us to carve out wasteful care, products and services that are unnecessary to the patient and that undermine value creation. Importantly, this principle is valid along the entire care delivery chain: for pharma and academia developing new care, providers delivering that care, payers paying for that care, policy regulating that care, and finally patients receiving that care.

You may ask: what has happened in the last twenty years since this was first established and why hasn't it been adopted more broadly?

In my personal experience of three decades at the forefront of health care, I came to notice several reasons for the poor adoption of VBHC. They are of technical, behavioral and cultural dimensions. Let's have a look, step by step, and see what potential can unfold once we see the opportunities for broad adoption at the end.

To start with, let's clarify some basic understandings.

Figure 3.2. The Matterhorn: simple from afar, complex on closer look.

Value-based health care is both very simple and very complex.

I was recently asked to describe VBHC in one word, and I was spontaneously thinking of the Matterhorn. It is one of the most "simple" and clearly visible mountain peaks that I know of. However, on closer inspection, getting up there is incredibly complicated and hard. And it takes teamwork.

Translated to VBHC, technically speaking, it is quite simple because it is built on three straightforward principles, as shown in figure 3.3:

1. Defining *outcomes* that matter to patients;
2. Regrouping those patients with similar medical conditions and who share the same needs into one *population* for which we want to measure these outcomes; and

3. Determining a well-defined *timeframe* in which these outcomes will be measured.

Figure 3.3. The pyramid of VBHC principles.

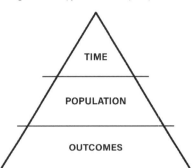

In order to define value, we need data. Data on outcomes, and data on cost. Data from individual patient charts, and data from populations of patients sharing the same needs. For this, we need to design technical IT infrastructure that we did not have in our legacy analog systems. Doing VBHC at scale through paper, fax and pen? Impossible. Further, we need to align on: which health outcomes to measure, and which patients to regroup into one population. This entails a complex multi-stakeholder process. It demands patients, physicians, and pharmacists, as well as provider administrators such as hospitals, insurers and other payers, to work hand-in-glove and to find enough common ground to agree on those definitions. The policymaker will also need to consider the respective laws and regulations that enable this essential switch in the payer system from services and products to outcomes and value. The beauty is that by working together on these common definitions whilst keeping the North on the patient, it naturally changes the dialogue – from a focus on cost to a focus on patients. Integrated ways of working lead to better human connections, which leads to the restoration of trust. Therefore, we can conclude that the purpose of VBHC is to remove obstacles and encourage certain behaviors. The empathetic focus on patient outcomes then creates an environment of trust.

As much as these principles are simple in theory, their implementation is highly complex. And they take time. Since it means pulling levers on multiple levels, by multiple stakeholders, it cannot be accomplished in one go or by one actor.

The encouraging news is that in several places, despite this complexity, these simple principles are already becoming a reality and shifting the needle toward better outcomes and better financials, too.

Let's look at a series of examples in the following section.

IT IS WORKING AND HERE IS HOW

We have seen that meeting patients' needs lies at the center of any sustainable value-based system of care. Hence the question: how can we consistently turn the patient journey into a satisfactory experience? In an increasingly value-centered world, personal choices around lifestyle and health management are only a fingertip away. Supporting people to better understand these choices is a centerpiece on the journey to bringing VBHC to fruition. Yet, given the complexity and fragmentation of the care delivery chain, both enhanced *patient empowerment* and a better level of *care coordination* are relevant components in a value-centered system of care. Additionally, acknowledging that health outcomes overall are influenced twice as much by *social determinants* than by clinical components, it is crucial to take a holistic look at the patient journey along the *health continuum*.

The following series of real-life examples from various geographies have actually shown that this fundamental transformation from volume to value is feasible. What they all have in common is that they highlight how, by putting the patient back at the center of the value chain, the transformation from a convoluted and fragmented care system to an integrated and coordinated care system is not only the right thing to do, but also leads to economic gains and system efficiencies.

Eventually, the North Star will be when all actors are rewarded based on how healthy a population is.

Sounds too good to be true? Let me show you that this is actually working and has become a reality in many parts of the world already.

The following paragraphs are structured around four patient-centric dimensions that continuously allow us to move the needle from fee-for-service to value-based health care (figure 3.4):

1. **Patient empowerment** (from reactive to proactive)
2. **Care coordination** (from redundancy to synergy)

3. **Health continuum** (from fixing to preventing)
4. **Social determinants of health** (from clinical to societal)

Figure 3.4. Four patient-centric dimensions to implement the three core VBHC principles.

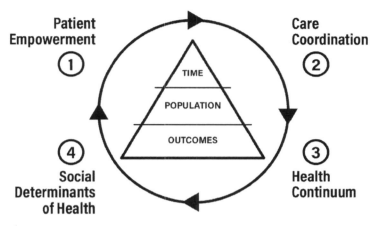

Patient empowerment (from reactive to proactive)

As highlighted by Hanna, an empowered patient and investments in health literacy beyond clinical care only represent an untapped potential to re-gain efficiencies. She asks, *"If my doctor only looks at billing the minutes of our conversation, how can we carve out quality time to talk about what's really important to me and what I really need?"*

Not enough time spent with patients, and therefore only fifty-five percent of recommended preventive measures effectively being delivered to patients, was among the motivators for the team at Oak Street Health (OSH) to completely shift their business model away from rewarding services in an FFS model to paying for how healthy their population is in a VBHC model.[87,88] *"From day one, our goal was simple: to keep patients happy, healthy, and out of the hospital,"* says Griffin Myers, OSH's Chief Medical Officer.[89] OSH brings comprehensive primary care services to underserved elderly communities in the American Midwest. Patients are managed within multi-disciplinary teams that are co-located in the same facility, and key performance parameters – such as visit and medication adherence and health outcomes – are jointly followed using a dashboard system. This not only provides transparency and fosters communication and trust, but also represents their common basis for incentives and payments.

What does this look like practically?

Very specifically, the team at OSH not only includes clinical components in their patient care plans, but, importantly, also social aspects.

They also invest in the education of their patients to empower them to fully understand their diagnosis and treatments, and how they can contribute to their own health management.

This means a fair portion of responsibility falls to the patient. In this model, depending on their socioeconomic status, patients are covered for transportation costs as the correlation between missed appointments and medication adherence had been shown to have a negative impact on patient outcomes. However, paying for transportation comes with an expectation to adhere to visit schedules, and OSH goes as far as publicly reporting both provider and patient compliance to the jointly agreed-upon care plans. In order to further tailor care plans, the education and intensity of visit schedules is stratified according to four distinct patient populations, depending on their level of sickness and immobility: well, average, sick and very sick (figure 3.5).

Figure 3.5. OSH patient population risk stratification.

	PATIENT	TIER	%PATIENTS	FOCUS
4	Very sick	Critical	4%	Speciality, avoid readmission, caregiver
3	Sick	Serious	25%	Family coordination, avoid readmission
2	Average	Fair	41%	Secondary prevention
1	Well	Good	30%	Preventive care, primary prevention

Source: Adapted from Porter et al, HBR case (2017)[88]

This patient stratification allows OSH not only to tailor treatments, but also to specify patients' educational needs and ability for self-management.

Furthermore, what this example showcases is the degree of cross-functional team coordination. Within the multi-stakeholder team, the individual assignment for each patient is done in close cooperation between physicians, nurses, caregivers, social workers, and the patient and their family (figure 3.6). Visit cadence and care plans are adapted accordingly. For specific and highly prevalent conditions in this population, such as hypertension, the multi-disciplinary team determines the range of target blood pressure levels in a given timeframe for each of the four strata of patients. Depending on how well these pre-defined, evidence-based results are met, rewards for all participants are structured accordingly.

Overall, this highly integrated modus operandi – a multi-disciplinary team with the patient at the center – has led to a staggering forty-one percent reduction in the rate of hospitalization.

As a result, patients were able to stay home more and longer, which in turn had a positive impact on cost efficiencies. Cost savings were subsequently redeployed in other areas, such as educational efforts and being able to take on more patients within the provider network.

Figure 3.6. Based on the OSH care model, the empowered patient at the center.

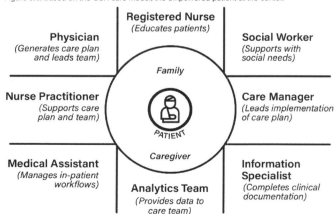

Care coordination (from redundancy to synergy)
Cross-functional care coordination is a common pillar across all

successful VBHC projects. In eleven OECD countries surveyed in 2016, between twenty-nine percent and fifty-one percent of people said they experienced problems of care coordination in a health service.[90]

However, new care models are emerging in several regions and countries. Two examples, which are outpacing many others in terms of perfection of care coordination, are in the therapeutic areas of diabetes and rheumatoid arthritis (RA).

The first one I'd like to mention and that has deeply impressed me is the Dutch-certified Diabeter multi-stakeholder consortium.[91] It has been created to focus on the specific needs and tailored care of children, adolescents and adults suffering from type 1 diabetes. As outlined in Hanna's story, this is a life-threatening disease that is usually diagnosed at an infant age, leaving families helpless in light of the complexity and urgency of needs. The only way to survive this is for patients and families to learn how to self-inject insulin on a daily basis. As recounted by Hanna, troubles adapting, problems at school and mental stress, coupled with frequent ER visits, are the norm. A greater level of coordination is required to prevent this from happening.

Hanna's vision of the empowered patient within a coordinated team means the patient is sitting at the center of a proverbial round table. In her case, this table would include an endocrinologist, a diabetes educator, a nurse, a podologist, an ophthalmologist, a personal trainer and a mental coach. The composition will vary depending on each patient's individual needs. All these professionals around the table need to be informed of, and aligned with, the patient's goals. As Hanna reflects,

"Ultimately, they need to be in the right spirit of co-creating these goals with me. I actually need to trust that these are the right goals for me, and believe it is worth my time and effort working on them."

This is precisely what both the Diabeter and the Oak Street Health multi-disciplinary networks deliver. Within integrated patient units (IPUs), they regroup providers, families, social workers and other relevant specialists.[92,93] IPUs act as a team that takes care of the patient collectively, rather than a parallel set of specialists acting in isolation, creating redundancy and ultimately driving cost. Within these IPUs, definitions and goals for outcomes are collectively assigned, measured and monitored in a transparent manner by using a central dashboard system. Importantly, the patient can remotely contribute by entering their health data, such as blood glucose level, insulin dosing or other pre-defined parameters of wellbeing, into a common digital platform. As a consequence, children covered within this network are far less likely to be admitted to the ER than they used to be.

Consequently, one can directly depict and analyze per patient what the cost reductions are on a full cycle of care.

Translating value to patients into value for the system: In 2018, the Diabeter model led to an overall saving of €9.6 million, as well as a fifty percent reduction in per-patient cost (from €7,350 to

€3,270) on an annual basis. The similar care coordination project ParkinsonNet yielded an overall €46.5 million and a reduction of €4,080 to €3,550 per patient.[94,95] The main clinical correlation of these cost savings is clinically meaningful delays of disease progression, complications and disabilities.

To exemplify the multi-stakeholder reach beyond patient and provider, in 2019 Diabeter signed a ten-year value-based contract with a Dutch insurer focusing on both short-term and long-term patient outcome goals (for example, short-term blood glucose levels and long-term organ damage linked to diabetes). All actors in this consortium are rewarded based on whether pre-defined outcomes are met and adapted to comply with a bonus-malus-system.[89]

In the context of type 2 diabetes, which is acquired and occurs later in life, the American Diabetes Association is leading the way to create a common platform of standards for adult patients that every care team is encouraged to follow.[96] Importantly, figure 3.7 showcases that these guidelines are not to be understood as fixed algorithms by which every patient has to follow the exact same procedures. Quite the contrary.

The whole sense of value-based care lies in the individualization of care and uses a standardized sets of guiding questions and principles.

Another example of care organization is the 'Joint Value' network of primary care and specialist providers that aims to optimize the health continuum of patients suffering from inflammatory joint

Figure 3.7. Diabetes Care Coordination Model from the American Diabetes Association.

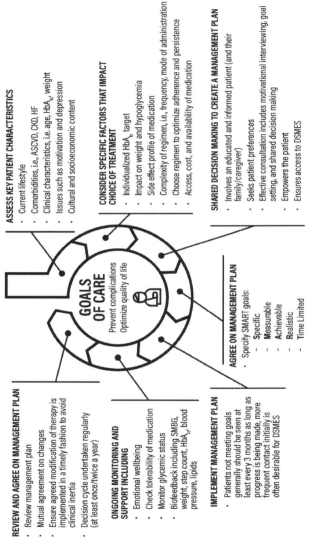

ASSESS KEY PATIENT CHARACTERISTICS
- Current lifestyle
- Comorbidities, i.e., ASCVD, CKD, HF
- Clinical characteristics, i.e. age, HbA_{1c}, weight
- Issues such as motivation and depression
- Cultural and socioeconomic content

CONSIDER SPECIFIC FACTORS THAT IMPACT CHOICE OF TREATMENT
- Individualized HbA_{1c} target
- Impact on weight and hypoglycemia
- Side effect profile of medication
- Complexity of regimen, i.e., frequency, mode of administration
- Choose regimen to optimize adherence and persistence
- Access, cost, and availability of medication

SHARED DECISION MAKING TO CREATE A MANAGEMENT PLAN
- Involves an educated and informed patient (and their family/caregiver)
- Seeks patient preferences
- Effective consultation includes motivational interviewing, goal setting, and shared decision making
- Empowers the patient
- Ensures access to DSMES

REVIEW AND AGREE ON MANAGEMENT PLAN
- Review management plan
- Mutual agreement on changes
- Ensure agreed modification of therapy is implemented in a timely fashion to avoid clinical inertia
- Decision cycle undertaken regularly (at least once/twice a year)

ONGOING MONITORING AND SUPPORT INCLUDING
- Emotional wellbeing
- Check tolerability of medication
- Monitor glycemic status
- Biofeedback including SMBG, weight, step count, HbA_{1c}, blood pressure, lipids

IMPLEMENT MANAGEMENT PLAN
- Patients not meeting goals generally should be seen at least every 3 months as long as progress is being made, more frequent contact initially is often desirable for DSMES

AGREE ON MANAGEMENT PLAN
- Specify SMART goals:
  - Specific
  - Measurable
  - Achievable
  - Realistic
  - Time Limited

GOALS OF CARE
Prevent complications
Optimize quality of life

ASCVD = Atherosclerotic Cardiovascular Disease
CKD = Chronic Kidney Disease
HF = Heart Failure
DSMES = Diabetes Self-Management Education and Support
SMBG = Self-Monitored Blood Glucose

disease, or rheumatoid arthritis (RA).[97] This medical condition is characterized by severe episodes of painful joint inflammation, slowly destroying bones and joints, leaving patients at a high risk of serious disabilities in the long run. In this integrated practice network, specialists, GPs and hospitals provide both episodic and preventive care in a highly coordinated fashion. Their mission is to provide the right care for patients living with RA at the right place and at the right time. With this in mind, they cover the whole patient journey within three dimensions: early access, personalized outcomes and life-long monitoring.

Notably, this is a good example of how the work of the ICHOM (International Consortium for Health Outcomes Measurement) is implemented in real life.[98,99] Based on the initial publication by Michael Porter and colleagues, these measurements provide standard sets to uniformly code outcome measures and therefore allow fully interoperable measurements between providers. With a particular focus on chronic diseases and the prevention of complications, it is a rich open source for anyone who aims to establish value-based principles in their environment. If you are interested, I highly encourage you to become familiar with these sets of broadly validated outcome definitions.

Although the Netherlands and the United States are somewhat spearheading efforts around value-based health care, there are many other projects and countries following suit.

Health continuum (from fixing to preventing)

The two examples in this section come from Scandinavia and South America.

In light of the three megatrends of the future – aging, chronic illnesses and mental health – the individual health continuum is coming into focus. In an increasingly value-based world, health care is not only about a patient's illness. It is also about preventing complications in the first place, protecting a person's health and enabling optimal quality of life. In other words, it is about life as a whole.

As we have seen earlier, our legacy FFS systems did not have a built-in incentive to reward healthy living. Although the paradigm shift to prevention has long been recognized as essential to improve overall health, there was little investment into preventive care and initiatives to keep people in a home environment all their lives, whether healthy or sick (figure 3.8). There simply was no business model demonstrating a positive return-on-investment for the notion of "not fixing something." VBHC holds the potential to reverse that trend. Shifting our systems from a "fix and repair" to a "prevent and maintain" mindset will allow us to consider health as one continuity. Acknowledging that there is no real binary endpoint in a person's life, other than birth and death, everything else being interconnected along the journey of life, health and illnesses.

Protecting healthy living, rather than receiving health care, is the true silver lining in a VBHC world.

This is what the Nordic Health 2030 Movement is doing differently.[100] By virtue of proactively allocating an equal five percent GDP spending on both preventive care and therapeutic care, this program is setting a precedent. Within a ten-year plan, they are taking a holistic view along the full health continuum to include prevention, behavioral and lifestyle changes as well as acute and chronic care. Co-created by more than thirty stakeholders, this public-private consortium aims to reorient and rebalance health care expenditure toward the early part of the health continuum. What the countries involved in this movement accomplish is innovation in health care on three levels: seeking synergies across multiple countries; building bridges across the public and private sectors; and proactively involving the policymaker. It beautifully exemplifies how a parallel top-down *and* a bottom-up approach can go hand-in-hand.

Framed by a governmental-endorsed 2030 strategy, projects by providers, payers and patients are emerging from the grassroots.

This is a beautiful example of how the seemingly inconceivable task of transforming a health care system from FFS to VBHC is undertaken in reality. It also demonstrates that this is not done in one go, but that it requires resilience and a long-term vision. What makes this project unique, in my eyes, is the visionary setting of re-allocating funds along the health continuum over time. Recalibrating the priorities from *therapeutic* care to *preventive* care requires multiple stakeholders to cooperate. By overcoming the silo mentality and positional bargaining, they set forth a path to amplify value with all stakeholders, potentially reaping the benefits for patients and society more broadly.

Figure 3.8. The health continuum.

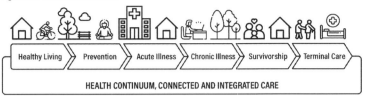

At the latter end of that health continuum, the Programa Contigo is an impressive success story of how VBHC principles can effectively help the most vulnerable: terminally ill patients and their families. *"Dying is not a medical event, but a human experience,"* is the mantra of the Colombia-based Keralty team, which established this program following a desperate experience by one of the founders, Dr Gabriela Sarmento.[101] Gabriela's father passed away in great pain and suffering, without much help and support for him and his family from the ecosystem around him. Realizing that this is generally the fate of eight in ten people, she decided to train as a doctor and become a palliative care specialist.

"We cannot avoid dying," Gabriela says. *"But the end of life doesn't have to be miserable."* Concerned about the quality of life during the latter part of the health continuum, and acknowledging that a disproportionate amount of money is spent during the last six months of a patient's terminal illness, the team at Keralty established a substantial new approach.

Contigo means "together". Within their people-centered care model, they meet patients in their homes and seek to address their physical, emotional, social and spiritual needs.

In only four years, sixteen mobile interdisciplinary teams have served over 3,600 patients. Patient satisfaction, symptom relief and wellbeing parameters have all scored highly in this relatively short period, with seventy-eight percent reporting full pain control, seventy-six percent feeling well and, overall, ninety-eight percent feeling comfortable. Because end-of-life support can be a traumatic experience, Keralty helps families create a more caregiving environment for their dying loved ones. With this support network in place, the team has achieved an overall satisfaction rate of ninety-eight percent, with sixty percent of patients able to stay home.

In addition to generating value to patients and their families, Programa Contigo has reduced health care expenditure for terminally ill patients by thirty percent, or $4 million.

The team at Keralty is driven by purpose and passion. Their motivation is to reduce patient suffering, bring back patient dignity and increase patient wellbeing. Focus on the patient and their outcomes, and the rest will follow: integrated teams, value to society and economic gains.

Social determinants of health (from clinical to societal)

Health is so much more than absence of illness. Many things in life interfere with our health.

If we truly aim to capture a person's health holistically, we need to expand our views beyond the clinical care component. Treating acute and chronic illness is important, but responding to people's needs outside of the exam room – from an emotional, socioeconomic and mental health point of view – is equally important.

Taking into account a patient's family and lifestyle choices, as well as workplace realities, can have a significant impact on the effectiveness of treatment options. Research shows that social determinants of health (SDOH) are five times more impactful on health outcomes than health care with traditional medicines and procedures.

What does that mean?

The analysis in figure 3.9 demonstrates the top five categories of factors that have been universally recognized as main influencers on our health.

Figure 3.9. SDOH impact compared to health care spending.

SDOH	HEALTH IMPACT	SPEND
Behavior	38%	$260 million
Socioeconomic	23%	$1,562 million
Biology	21%	$15 million
Medical	11%	$3,337 million
Environment	7%	$400 million

Source: Adapted from www.goinvo.com including global data sources.[102]

Looking more closely at the table in figure 3.9, what is most striking is the discrepancy between the drivers of health impact versus the amount of money spent on each.[102] Eighty-nine percent of the factors that influence our health are *not* related to pills and other medical interventions. Rather, they're related to the way we live and work, what our intrinsic biology and our extrinsic environment dictate, and, finally, where we were born, how we were raised and the type of education we received.

*We substantially overspend in areas with the
smallest impact and dramatically underspend
in areas with the biggest impact.*

More precisely, in this example, we are investing over $3 trillion on products, services and procedures that account for a minority (eleven percent) of health impacts. This is ten times more money than we invest in behavioral aspects, which account for thirty-eight percent of the impacts on our health, and twice as much as we spend on socioeconomic aspects, which account for twenty-three percent. To put it simply, we are ready to spend (waste?) $100 on medical interventions to fix illnesses, but this money and these interventions have only limited impact on our overall health. In contrast, we only spend one dollar on lifestyle and behavioral changes to prevent illness and other health complications in the first place. This example shows where and how we invest our health care dollar, and how much this has outgrown any proportionality and common sense.

In an ideal world, the numbers in the right-hand column of figure 3.9 should be correlating better with those in the left-hand column. This is what a strategy like the Nordic Health 2030 Movement aims to do. Efforts need to focus on rebalancing the medical and socioeconomic factors in order to foster better health prevention and more effectively tailor health care. Employers, pharmaceutical companies, educators and health professionals need to be involved.

Efforts and investments should be redirected to socioeconomic levers of health, including workplace set-ups and behaviors;

educational programs influencing behavioral changes relating to smoking habits, nutrition, movement, exercise and sleep patterns; and tailored initiatives supporting populations at biological or hereditary risk. Let's have a look at the example of a thirty-year-old: someone with less than an upper secondary education level can expect to live for five and a half *fewer* years than someone with a university degree or equivalent. The difference is even more pronounced in men than women, with an average gap of 6.9 years for men compared to four years for women, as assessed in 2019 across twenty-six OECD countries.[10]

Health is mostly managed outside of health care. It requires effective trans-sector dialogue and cooperation.

The OECD's *Promoting Health, Preventing Disease, the Economic Case* shows how much of the socioeconomic inequalities could be preventable.[103] For this to occur effectively, the authors stipulate that intersectoral policy strategies are required, reaching beyond the departments of health. Many critical social determinants of health lie outside of health systems, in areas like transport safety, environmental and urban planning, business regulation, education and fiscal policy. As to how to promote good health and disease prevention in a more cost-effective way, the authors suggest *"regular face-to-face dialogue between policymakers and so-called 'knowledge brokers', who act as intermediaries familiar with both the research and policymaking environments."* As much as this is an important step for trans-sector dialogue on a governmental level, I find it also highly relevant to the five decision makers in health care. What about regular forum meetings between the five main actors – with or without a knowledge broker – to nurture this cross-sector dialogue from and within health care?

FOCUS ON THE PATIENT AND
THE REST WILL FOLLOW

It is really encouraging to see how VBHC projects lead to improved patient outcomes and enhanced satisfaction across the ecosystem, and also how VBHC triggers significant economic gains. As such, implementing VBHC is one of the major levers required to restore the imbalance between innovation and affordability. As we have seen, VBHC provides exactly what we have been missing in an FFS world: transparency, ownership and accountability along a full cycle of care.[92] A recent comparative analysis of four health systems is demonstrating that VBHC, using the so-called time-driven activity-based costing (TDABC) method, enables transparent cost assessments. *"With this approach, the actual costs of delivering care to a patient with a certain condition are measured from the bottom up, by looking into what happens to a patient in the course of a treatment and what specific costs of all processes are associated with it."*[104]

Start small, identify a test project, run a pilot study – you choose. Know that many small projects can move the needle, as seen in the Dutch set of VBHC projects.

One of the leading groups of practitioners supporting real-world implementation of value-based principles is the VBHC Center Europe, working closely with ICHOM and scholars at Harvard Business School. Chairman Dr Fred van Eenennaam describes the essence and simplicity of VBHC beautifully: *"Let the teams focus on outcomes and cost will follow."* During one of the group meetings, he presented the example of *"the resilience of the Dutch health care system."* If you're interested in implementing outcomes-based reward models, I invite you to watch his brief yet powerful video presentation.[95] He outlined that in the Netherlands alone, if no change occurs, health care expenditure is forecast to grow from €90 billion in 2020 to €175 billion in 2040. However, by introducing VBHC, the Netherlands was able to start bending that curve. Over the course of 2019, 173 known smaller VBHC pilot projects incurred substantial savings as a whole of at least €1 billion. Of note, the majority of these projects were grassroots initiatives, taken by local providers and payer networks. It is predicted that the ongoing transformation toward VBHC continues to shave off economic gains to the tune of €25 billion. As such, even a multitude of smaller projects showcases the power to break the trend of overspending and, as such, can restore the balance between innovation and affordability locally.

As we are witnessing the radical shift of power from the provider (doctor) to the consumer (patient), moving forward, patients will be the ones choosing providers, payers and medicines based on what and who will deliver the most value to them.

In summary, customer-centricity, outcomes-focus and value-based principles also work in health care. But it takes time. If you're interested in learning more, you may find some helpful guiding questions in the supplementary materials on page 235 as you seek to determine whether VBHC may work in your environment. Note that the magic unfolds once VBHC starts catalyzing teamwork around the collective North Star: aiming for results that matter to patients. The possible consequences are massive, both economically and culturally. What has changed – since the early days of Michael Porter bringing the concept to health care – is that we now hold the technology tools to process the massive amount of health data needed to measure a full cycle of care, as you shall see in the following chapter.

TOP TAKEAWAYS FROM CHAPTER THREE

☑ Individual leaders who find other likeminded, risk-taking leaders can trigger a significant movement that improves the patient experience and economic gains. VBHC works in conjunction with bottom-up initiatives and top-down leadership support, spanning across the five main actors in health care: patients, providers, pharma, payers and policymakers.

☑ The focus on both societal and clinical health outcomes across the whole health continuum, integrated care coordination, and the fundamental switch of incentives from volume to value, carry massive potential to address the imbalance of innovation and affordability.

☑ Patient centricity and patient empowerment are the keys to unlock resilient systems of health. VBHC is the theoretical framework, and digital provides the tools to make this happen operationally, as you will see in the following chapter.

CHAPTER 4

Acquiring a digital footprint to eliminate inefficiencies and foster cooperation

"There is nothing like a dream to create the future."

~VICTOR HUGO

SMART SOLUTIONS BRING BACK
THE HUMAN TOUCH

A few years ago, I personally experienced how fragmentation and redundancies lead to errors and frustrations. It was in the context of a planned vacation to Asia that required checking the potential need for infection prophylaxis for diseases such as malaria.

I was at the tropical medicine institute within a major academic institution in Switzerland. Over five hours, I repeated five times the same general information – including my date of birth, my place of birth, my list of illnesses, my list of medications and my emergency contacts – to five different people. Sound familiar?

It left me feeling like a broken record when I returned to see my own patients in the afternoon.

After this wasted half-day, filled mostly with waiting periods and navigating the hospital's corridors, reception desks and check-in counters, I realized there had actually not been enough time to engage in a really meaningful discussion with any of the health professionals I dealt with. Instead of learning about risks and behavioral measures that could have helped me mitigate infection risks during the trip in the first place, I experienced a rather mechanical and impersonal interaction with the nurse-on-duty who was mostly concentrating on her computer, hardly looking at me, and making me feel like a robot rather than a patient seeking medical advice. I was distracted when I heard her say that, in addition to malaria prophylaxis, I needed another hepatitis A shot.

What this experience demonstrates is the lack of an integrated value chain from start to finish.

The scoop came one week later, when my GP notified me that the hep A vaccine was done just one year earlier and marked in my vaccination booklet, which the nurse must have overlooked despite being so focused on getting all the documentation right and in order. In short, the important information had become lost amidst redundant administrative tasks.

Despite feeling frustrated, I also felt empathy for the nurse.

Too often have I been in exactly the same seat: an overly bureaucratic machine requiring me to spend my time on documenting and billing, and not leaving me with enough time for my patients. However, after this experience, I was left thinking, "I am healthy and fit; this was just a wasted morning, nothing of real importance.

How does an ill patient actually deal with this? Feeling dizzy, uncomfortable and otherwise in distress, how can they possibly navigate the seemingly endless corridors and paperwork, and avoid duplicate tests and treatments? How does it feel when you are sick but are not able to have meaningful discussions with your doctor and don't feel that you are actually being cared for?"

Patients *and* physicians want more *quality* time *together.*

In an environment of fragmentation, redundancy and wasteful care delivery, time becomes a commodity. Time wastage, unnecessary bureaucracy and bridging the gaps in legacy hospital facilities are the key challenges faced by actors within an ineffective FFS system.

How can we overcome the fragmentation in health care? What if we could find a way to bring back the gift of time and the human touch?

Interestingly, the answer to these questions lies in technology. You may be thinking, "A tech solution to satisfy a human need? How could this possibly work?"

---

*Health care is all about connections – digital
is catalyzing these for the benefit of patients.
All we need to do is acquire the right
digital literacy to make it a reality.*

In health care, the potential utilities of digital are multifold. From processing high-volume images in radiology, pathology and dermatology to interventional support in domains such as cardiology and ophthalmology, the field is only in its infancy. Dr Eric Topol has written about novel technologies in health care in his seminal book, *Deep Medicine: How Artificial Intelligence Can Make Health Care Human Again.*[105] Digitalization is about simplifying processes. By using machines and technology, we can bring back time in the doctor-patient relationship. Digital, artificial intelligence (AI) and machine learning (ML) are alleviating workloads by automating processes and streamlining communication channels.

Health care has been late to this show, though.

It is the least digitized industry, and it feels like the most disconnected one. While many other industries have long since upgraded their systems and infrastructure to facilitate data exchange and automated data processing, health care has been stuck with paper charts and fax machines, and legacy systems that do not communicate with each other, resulting in information loss and errors.

But the good news is that health care is catching up. And it is catching up fast. The COVID-19 pandemic has only accelerated this digital transformation.

One example is telehealth.

During the pandemic, embracing telehealth was a blessing, as it helped reduce the burden on providers and enhanced access for patients to services during periods of social distancing. Telehealth is not a new concept, though. In 1925, the cover of *Science and Invention* featured a doctor who tele-diagnosed a patient with an imaginary teledactyl that would allow him to touch base with the patient at home.[106] It would take another century for the Institute of Medicine in the US to recognize telemedicine as an important evolving area to innovate care delivery.[107] For the last sixty years, teleradiology, telepathology and telemedicine have been emerging to bridge the barriers of distance and time between clinicians and patients. For example, a three-year randomized controlled trial in England found that telehealth reduced emergency admissions by twenty percent and emergency attendance by fifteen percent for patients with chronic conditions, including diabetes, obstructive pulmonary disease and heart failure.[108]

However, what prior generations were lacking was the right technology to scale, the right incentive to change, or the right context to overcome a "this can't be done" mentality.

There are distinct advantages that make the digital transformation so essential to health care: it not only fosters interconnectivity, but also provides the means to eliminate inefficiencies and restore the human touch in medicine.

Telemedicine, just like video conferencing, was available to us way before this pandemic hit. But it wasn't in our habits and it wasn't used broadly. This is partly because it wasn't "billable". A doctor's appointment over the phone or video simply wasn't reimbursable with the insurance. Make no mistake; it wasn't the fault of the payer or the provider, there simply was no system and framework that would allow such a transaction. However, when there is a collective sense of urgency, it can unlock real transformation and change in behavior. Translated into numbers, the COVID-19 pandemic has spurred a flurry of investments into this new sector of telehealth, with the start-up community having raised a record $3.3 billion in funding globally in the last quarter of 2020 alone.[109]

Figure 4.1. The interconnected world of digital in health care.

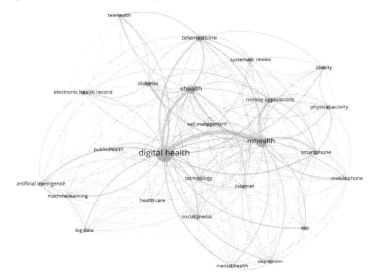

Source: Courtesy Marius Mainz.[110]

Before I move on to explore how digital revolutionizes health care, let me clarify what we actually mean by "digital" in health care. It seems to be such a buzz word these days, and seems to mean so many different things to so many different people. The upcoming breakout box summarizes some of the facts and fiction.

Generally speaking, digitally powered technology can be quite confusing. During the online research for this book, I came across a helpful network map of various interconnected keywords in the realm of digital and health. Out of 2,135 digital health publications, the network map in figure 4.1 shows keywords used by authors, which occurred twenty-five times or more, demonstrating the underlying interconnected structure in digital health research.

Later in this chapter, I will discuss a number of the terms you can see in the graph. But generally speaking, the most important clarification to make is between AI and digital health (D-Health).

The key distinction in health care is between AI and D-Health. They are two sides of the same (digital) coin. Complementary, yet distinct.

AI speaks to the automation of algorithms that can help make better predictions and assist users in tailored information gathering. D-Health describes the utilization of software applications, sensors and wearables that can be used for documentation purposes as well as diagnostic, preventive or therapeutic measures.

Let's go through each one of these aspects step by step, and let me share a few compelling examples for each along the way.

BREAKOUT BOX 2:
DIGITAL IN HEALTH CARE – FICTION VERSUS FACT

FICTION	FACT
• Is replacing humans, doctors or relationships	• Finds correlations in massive amounts of data that humans can't
• Artificial intelligence is capable of human-level intelligence or self-consciousness	• Compresses time and space for humans
• Performs complex semantic tasks	• Depends on input and data
• Understands complex natural language	• Is only as good as the humans governing it
• Replaces the human touch (medicine occurs at the intersection of science and art, so, in addition to data, it requires emotions and all senses – not only speaking, but also hearing, seeing, touching and smelling)	• Empowers people to own their own data and health
	• Brings massive efficiencies to health systems
	• Fosters connectivity between humans

ARTIFICIAL INTELLIGENCE IS MAKING
THE COMPLEX SIMPLE

Since the beginning of the new millennium, the internet has had a massive effect on our lives. It has opened up the floodgates to an overflow of infinite possibilities and information. Making sense of this new complexity, and making it play to our favor, is what digital and advanced analytics are all about. As such, AI and ML have entered our lives. We are not always aware of the insights that AI techniques extract from data on an everyday basis, but with each Google search, each Amazon order and each restaurant reservation via OpenTable, they facilitate our personalized choices.

Most of our social media platforms, be it Twitter, LinkedIn or Instagram, tailor the information flow in our personalized feeds using AI-powered techniques. In the hospital setting, smart robots with AI chatbot technology have been utilized during the pandemic to clean wards, deliver meals and dispense medication.[111,112] For personal care, solutions such as Ada Health are supporting better health outcomes and clinical excellence by assisting triage to deliver more appropriate care and patient empowerment.[113] For physicians specifically, Babylon Health aims to revolutionize health care by empowering doctors with AI.[114]

This is what smart digital solutions provide: information at the right time, at the right place, to whoever needs it.

In order to leverage the full potential of digital in health care, it is essential to clarify why we are using it in the first place. Buying software apps, developing wearables and investing in computer programs for the sake of it doesn't have any meaning in and of itself. In contrast, digital is *the* means to an end. It won't just magically solve all our problems, because digital tools per se don't bring value. Make no mistake: if not planned and coordinated carefully, there is real risk that this software tech explosion will further drive up costs, and lead to increased data privacy concerns and unnecessary care.

Digital can connect the pipes, but it can't clean the pipes.

Yes, automation is what is needed to clean up the nonsensical bureaucracy in the context of hospitals, insurers, drug development and public health. But AI can never replace humans when it comes to setting the right purpose. Instead, before launching into big investments, we must first focus on identifying underlying problems: for example, institutional discrepancies in communication and documentation processes; incompatible platforms; or legal and regulatory hurdles to data sharing. All of these "hardware" choices need to be made before embarking on large-scale software infrastructure projects.

Determining the right reason for the right, smart solution brings true progress in health care.

In my view, and following the guidance of many experts in the field, AI can indeed accelerate the transformation into a human-centric and value-based health care system.

What if there were a magical technology that could detect and predict cancer spread and assign a treatment that is tailored to you? What if it could help avoid illnesses and complications from chronic illness in the first place? What if there were a device that could help me decide when I need to see a doctor and when I can wait? Well, many of the tools to make this a reality already exist, and there are many real-life examples that show how we're changing the way we innovate in medical research and the way we deliver care. Let's look at a few examples around both the innovation and the care delivery aspects.

AI streamlines clinical research and makes health care innovation more efficient

AI is all about correlation. It helps humans whenever the amount of data is too massive to comprehend. It finds patterns in data that surpass the capacity of the human brain and senses. In health care and beyond, the sweet spot of artificial intelligence is whenever it is being combined with *human* intelligence. It helps humans to scale solutions that have existed before – but these solutions sometimes weren't used because they were too time-consuming or too resource-intensive.

There is one really important aspect to keep in mind: AI does not find the answers itself. It needs to be fed with information and data. In health care, these are patient-related data. However, these data are scattered across the various stakeholders in the ecosystem – either as very detailed individual patient data or within an amalgamation of basic data (stemming from wearables, electronic health records (EHRs) or prescriptions) to more complex data such as genomics and other biological data. Described as *big data*, these data can serve to develop tailored therapies and precision medicine.

The way AI can be utilized is to augment the human expertise in three dimensions: discovery of new drugs, precision of diagnostics and prediction of treatment outcomes.

In medicine, combining AI technology with clinical expertise is what holds true transformative power on the way to personalized medicine.

Someone who showcases this intersection between tech, science and the clinics perfectly is Dr Thomas Clozel, the CEO at the AI-powered life sciences company Owkin.[115] A hematologist by training, he realized the potential that the Fourth Industrial Revolution holds for medicine, science and drug development, and went on to found Owkin in 2016. In a discussion on my podcast podium #LetsTalkValue, he explains, *"You reap full potential once you start mixing knowledge: integrating health care experts together with software engineers and AI experts."*[116] Specifically, Owkin's mission is to optimize medical research and drug development with the power of AI: identifying biomarkers, predicting outcomes, optimizing clinical trial designs, and enhancing patient selection to ultimately influence patient outcomes.

Instead of trying to reconcile different data sources from hospital A, B and C, which carry the risk of not being compatible because of different data coding, different data quality and different patient-level data content, Owkin applies federated artificial intelligence (FedAI). This elegantly circumvents the need to reconcile raw datasets from different locations. The way it works is by using one hospital for testing a new AI algorithm (training set) and validation datasets in another hospital. This technique allows you to develop algorithms in one homogenous environment of one hospital and then only transfer the algorithm, not the raw data. In the next hospital, the algorithm then becomes further refined, as outlined in figure 4.2.

This federated approach not only leverages various locations to sequentially evolve AI algorithms, but it also elegantly eliminates data privacy concerns. If patient-level data needed to be transferred from one hospital to another, that would require patient approval. Transferring only the algorithm from one place to another is what FedAI delivers. To complicate things further, various hospitals use different IT infrastructures that do not necessarily communicate with each other. Therefore, in today's analog legacy systems, grouping data from different hospitals is simply not feasible, even outside of data privacy concerns. AI powered solutions hold the promise to overcome all of these hurdles.

Figure 4.2. Owkin's FedAI methodology manages structural, legal and geographic barriers.

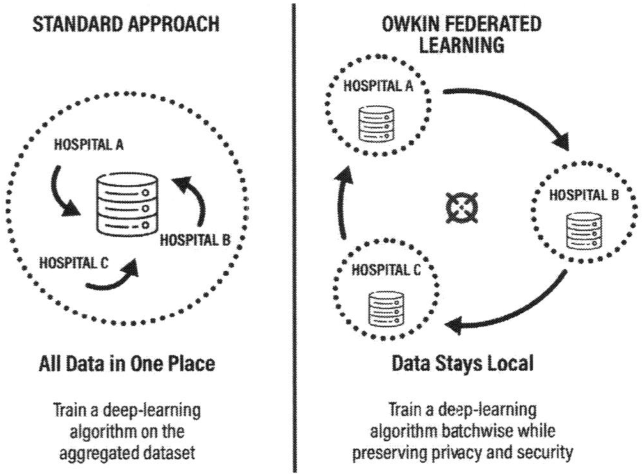

STANDARD APPROACH

HOSPITAL A

HOSPITAL B

HOSPITAL C

All Data in One Place

Train a deep-learning algorithm on the aggregated dataset

OWKIN FEDERATED LEARNING

HOSPITAL A

HOSPITAL B

HOSPITAL C

Data Stays Local

Train a deep-learning algorithm batchwise while preserving privacy and security

Source: owkin.com/federated-learning/

Three real-life examples of applied FedAI are the HealthChain consortium across four hospitals, the Melloddy public-private partnership for drug discovery, as well as the Mesonet digital pathology model for mesothelioma, which makes molecular predictions from traditional histopathology samples.

The HealthChain consortium, launched in June 2018, received a €10 million grant from a French public investment bank and has gathered together two AI start-ups, four large academic institutions, as well as the Substra Foundation.[117] The aim is to collaboratively gain new insights in dermato-oncology, pathology and fertility by using advanced analytics across public and private actors.

The large-scale international platform MELLODDY, under the auspices of the Innovative Medicines Initiative (IMI), aims to leverage decentralized data from ten pharmaceutical companies, analyzing their collections of small molecules to better predict efficiency in drug discovery without exposing proprietary information.[118]

Lastly, the new Mesonet classification model has demonstrated that by crowdsourcing datasets from various research institutions, this FedAI-powered analysis could extract new correlations by combining standard histology samples (stained tumor samples analyzed under the microscope) with clinical features.[119-120] More precisely, the superpower of this consortium and technique has identified the role of the microenvironment and tumor stroma to be predictive for the survival of patients suffering from this rare, asbestos-related cancer.

Similarly, in breast cancer, the *HE2RNA* model is able to predict molecular information from histology images alone whenever associated genetic tumor material is not available.[121] This provides a powerful tool to enhance clinical practice all the way from diagnosis to treatment optimization for breast cancer patients who may have limited diagnostic material available from their tumor removals.

----

*Connecting data and people is what the true
potential is. Once our infrastructure and*

*ways of working transition from analog to
digital, health care will be faster, cheaper and
safer, and we will feel more connected.*

As outlined in chapter two, currently drug development is a high-risk, high-cost endeavor and, overall, not very efficient in tailoring treatments for certain conditions. Therefore, using AI and ML screening platforms can boost both efficiency and success rates. There are numerous start-up companies in the private life sciences sector and academic research teams in the public sector, all advancing the potential of AI and ML to amplify the human intelligence of researchers and clinicians in developing better targeted diagnostics and treatments for patients. In the wake of the COVID-19 pandemic, global health care AI start-up funding reached a record high of over $2 trillion in the fourth quarter of 2020 alone.[109]

*AI can open the door to precision medicine, precision
diagnostics and precision prevention, which in turn
will make health care less wasteful and more efficient.*

This generates value on two levels.

On the one hand, transformative therapies can be tailored to those patients who will truly benefit from them. The before-mentioned chatbot AI technology brings intuitive and predictive medicine to the health continuum: from enhancing early disease detection to chronic disease management through symptom detection, reminders, and coordination of medicines, doctors' visits and refills of medicine. Payers, patients and health authorities are all likely to pay for its full value once they know that the end user truly derives better outcomes. On the other hand, it reduces waste because it spares patients from both the risk of misdiagnosis and unnecessary toxicity or ineffective treatments. This is the essence of precision medicine as an enabler for VBHC. AI predictive power will be an essential component of identifying new biomarkers, new drugs, and better drugs with fewer side effects.

AI brings VBHC to life and makes care delivery more efficient

As described in chapter three, the True North for health care is a system that incentivizes value and quality of health outcomes rather than volumes of services and procedures. The one big reason why VBHC has not seen more uptake, despite being known and well-described since the start of this millennium, is the lack of electronic data capture at the point of care: the patient.

Health happens at home.

From a patient perspective, health and health care start and end at home. This is where AI brings the health continuum and the patient journey closer into focus. In the expert community, the saying goes, "AI doesn't have legs." If AI were the brain and the patient data were the legs, you need to feed the brain with the data and find the data where the patient is.

In other words, being able to capture the data at point of care means capturing this data as early as in a patient's home environment via sensors, wearables and home monitoring machines. Remote patient monitoring (RPM) means capturing data where and when it really matters. There is huge untapped potential here. It also allows for better long-term follow-up and, as such, enables VBHC outcome drivers, as you have seen in the example of rheumatoid arthritis in chapter three. Additionally, from a clinical research perspective, during the COVID-19 pandemic, those researchers who were able to quickly pivot to AI-enabled patient recruitment and decentralized, virtual RPM were able to maintain their research activities virtually despite the lockdown disruptions.[122]

Digitalization is the fuel that ignites the value engine.

In the routine care setting, research has shown that RPM leads to significant reduction of mortality and re-hospitalization. In light of chronic illnesses such as heart disease, cancer, diabetes and Alzheimer's disease, which are globally touching six out of ten people, it is also a major cost driver.[123] Equivalent to nearly twenty percent of US GDP, it represents a massive potential for economic gains at the same time.[124] A randomized controlled study in Germany demonstrated that RPM in addition to usual care led to a significant drop of all-cause mortality for moderate to severely affected heart failure patients.[125] Not only is RPM highly impactful in helping patients manage their conditions and drive better outcomes, it has also been shown to be highly cost effective.[126] In the example of Optilys, a French organization that combines direct patient care with AI to deliver better solutions to patients in their homes, this has led to a fifty percent reduction of heart failure-related mortality, a one-third reduction in hospitalization needs, and savings of more than €5,000 per patient.[127]

Through the advent of AI and ML, we finally hold the enablers to move us to a value-based system of health. Generating results that matter to patients requires the ability to capture, measure, code and analyze those outcomes. In an analog world built on paper charts, faxes and mail delivery, this was impossible to achieve. Now, with the advent of digitalization, we hold the digital toolbox in our hands, enabling us to collect and process large amounts of data.

With the advent of digitalization, VBHC can finally be scaled through the electronic measurement of data, standardization of processes, and simplifying communication flows between all actors.

From a provider perspective, AI is also the magic button to facilitate physicians' workflows.

Remember my story about the visit at the tropical medicine institute? AI would have had the potential to transform that experience by bringing back time and the human touch to medicine. Rahul Varschneya, co-founder of the software development firm Arkenea, describes the potential for AI algorithms to help doctors and patients with a more comprehensive approach to disease management: *"Even when the disease is detected and classified, the treatment process can cause supplemental issues. A treatment plan does not simply include prescribing medicines and suggesting exercises, but* [should] *also help patients manage their treatment programmes, coordinate care plans, and consider the peril of an adverse event occurring."*[128]

Additionally, new AI-powered gadgets, such as medication adherence and refill reminder devices and apps, can be added to a doctor's toolbox. For example, during the COVID-19 crisis, a research and engineering team in Switzerland developed a smart stethoscope that predicts COVID-19 in nine out of ten patients based on a deep-breath algorithm from lung auscultations.[129] In parallel, AI algorithms from patient symptoms can predict disease progression based on patient symptom reporting. In the context of COVID-19, an Israeli research project demonstrated proof-of-concept that the combination of clinical symptom recording with molecular blood analysis can reliably contribute to lean health care resource utilization and lower the public health burden.[130,131]

In addition to disease prediction, AI technology can also assist with more efficient patient triage and determining which patients actually require a clinic visit.

In the case of oncology, cancer patients often suffer symptoms linked to their underlying cancer and related treatments. Fortunately, in many instances these can be mild, such as fatigue, loss of appetite, digestion issues or dermatologic symptoms. Therefore, they do not always require a doctor's visit or hospitalization right away, but yet have a significant impact on the patient's wellbeing and quality of life.

A study at the University of Leeds has demonstrated that cancer patients undergoing chemotherapy benefited from an AI-automated mobile device that helps to self-manage symptoms and assists with decision-making as to when to seek further medical attention.[132] Program lead Dr Galina Velikova concluded that *"remote online monitoring options have the potential to be a patient-centered, safe, and effective approach to support patients during cancer treatment and manage the growing clinical workload for cancer care."* To showcase the potential for both patients and the market, the company that developed Outcomes4Me was able to raise €4.7 million in 2020 alone with its one-stop-shop app, helping breast cancer patients *"who don't know what to do next."*[133]

From a hospital and academic perspective, digitalization brings transformation power at scale. Labeled as "smart hospitals," several provider networks and academic institutions are seizing the opportunity of AI, ML and D-Health to optimize their operations, staff satisfaction and patient experiences.

Internationally, there are two examples leading the way in scaling digitalization – to the point of revolutionizing both patient and health care worker experiences.

Firstly, in Germany, Essen University Hospital is embarking on a multi-year strategy that aims to utilize digitalization, AI and hardware technology to ease the administrative burden for physicians and nurses, and overall promote the wellbeing of patients.

"With the 'Smart Hospital' initiative, we want to achieve a real cultural change in the hospital

system that will benefit employees significantly
and optimize [care] for patients."[34]

They are breaking down silos by connecting the various parts and stakeholders within a hospital around common goals and patient health outcomes, all compatible with the implementation of VBHC principles. What strikes me most when watching their video on YouTube is the strong collaborative nature.[135] Their smart plan is taking both patients and hospital staff on a journey into the future of medical care by dissolving the top-down culture and replacing it with cross-functional decision-making within a diverse steering committee.

Secondly, in the US, the Mayo Clinic launched the SPARC Innovation Program (See, Plan, Act, Refine, Communicate) already some fifteen years ago. This is a cross-functional initiative placing the patient experience at the center of their transformation strategy.

"The way in which we deliver health care has remained
surprisingly static over the years. For example, the
relationship between physicians and their patients
has been largely paternalistic. Exam rooms today look
much as they always have. It's odd that in light of the
advancements in other parts of the medical process,
there's been very little change in these areas." [136]

The SPARC program was built on principles of design thinking, which includes prototyping of novel ideas within multi-disciplinary

teams, then applying insights from these prototypes and transferring them in rapid succession to new initiatives. It eventually led to
the institutionalization of innovation at Mayo Clinic in a dedicated
Center for Innovation (CFI).[137] Putting cooperation, strategic thinking and team spirit at the center of their efforts, the CFI's tagline
summarizes this new culture shift perfectly: *"Think Big. Start Small.
Move Fast.™"* By specifically dedicating resources, investments and
infrastructure to innovation, it allowed this hospital and academic
institution to combine experts in human-centered, innovative
design with real-world, VBHC professionals and patients. More
recently, Mayo launched the Clinical Data Analytics Platform,
enabling researchers to build AI and ML models to utilize insights
from data and develop new therapies, solve complex medical
problems, and improve the patient and clinician experience.[138]

As we have just seen, AI and ML can bring back the gift of time
by automating repetitive processes such as medication dispens-
ing, scheduling shifts and patient flows, and capturing patient
demographics, and make data sharing instant and interoperable
between patient, nurse, pharmacist and hospital administrator.

They also bring enormous potential to streamline and accelerate
the overall diagnostic and innovation process. For digital to realize
its full potential, data are essential.

Now, D-Health is what allows us to capture this data in the first
place.

Let's explore.

CONNECTING ANALOG PEOPLE
WITH DIGITAL SOLUTIONS

Essentially, and in many ways, we are analog creatures. We are not digital aliens. Our five senses are wired in the here and now, one emotion at a time. Our thoughts and emotions switch fast, and they come and go like a revolving door, but they are still sequential. In fact, multitasking is like a fast-paced, alternating current. It swaps thoughts and actions within milliseconds, but it is still analog and sequential. This is what the generation of "digital natives" does to perfection.

D-Health is a one-stop-shop that delivers care, information and communication to your fingertips in a direct-to-consumer fashion. It bridges our analog gaps with digital tools. And it does so in real time, twenty-four hours a day, seven days a week, with no delays. It connects data with people, people with people, and it can also directly interact with health and therefore impact outcomes. It allows for instant data sharing and serves as a connector between the top five actors in health care.

D-Health is the most important disruptor to transform a transactional and paternalistic culture into a set of smart and connected partnerships.

No wonder there is a high demand for digital solutions in health care. People are impatient in wanting to make progress and alleviate their daily struggles with inefficiencies. Somehow, digital is the new currency in health care. Even before the advent of the

COVID-19 pandemic, the global D-Health market represented an opportunity of approximately $350 billion, including many subcategories tailored to the health care consumer, such as diagnostics, prevention, research and development, health systems operations and care delivery.[139] As outlined in chapter one, the world of value is shifting toward the consumer, the customer experience and the end results that matter to people. In health care, this means reimagining the patient *and* the doctor as on-demand consumers.

Health on demand, and the power of the consumer, is what drives the culture change from fixing to preventing along the health continuum. What if digitalization could foster better health?

This is becoming a reality as we speak. It started before COVID-19 hit our world and, ever since, has seen a sharp acceleration. Stakeholders in the ecosystem – in the private and the public sector – are well advised to adapt to this change and stay ahead of the curve if they want to maintain a leadership role in this industry. Those who stick to old ways of analog, transactional and hierarchical relationships are unlikely to survive.

M-health is the next frontier in health care

What if there were a personalized platform where your health data was captured and instantly shared with your doctor, twenty-four hours a day, seven days a week? An open communication channel that could send health alerts in an emergency, and that would otherwise assist you on a daily basis to manage your health condition. (For example, getting quick answers on the spot to your questions on how best to respond to that high blood pressure, high blood sugar, and so on.) A way to avoid lengthy appointment waiting times and unnecessary trips to the clinic by instead receiving a simple answer, offered remotely, that could steer your daily health management in the right direction.

It is all at our doorsteps already.

Mobile health, or m-health, comes in the form of mobile devices, wearables and rapidly evolving sensor technology. In many ways, it accelerates the consumerization of health care. It allows people to track and share their sensor data, including self-reported symptoms (also referred as PROMS, patient reported outcome measures), and creates the ability to self-reward health management at large. It has long been in our lives, with many people wearing gadgets that track the number of steps per day, number of hours slept per night, or tracking heart beats when working out. You may actually be wearing one as you read this book. These devices are getting smaller and cheaper. Some sensors are even becoming biodegradable, and algorithms are becoming more powerful in their ability to predict medical outcomes.[140]

_____

The impact of m-health is threefold: it fosters patient empowerment; it moves the needle on the health continuum toward prevention and earlier intervention; and it leads to efficiencies in the system by reducing redundancies and delays in the care delivery cycle between provider and patient.

_____

M-health allows users to send alerts, notifications and reminders. It connects patients with providers and pharmacists (figure 4.3). It empowers people and drives lifestyle changes that are essential to move the needle on social determinants of health, as seen in chapter three.

Figure 4.3. The toolbox of m-health bringing patient empowerment and care coordination to life.

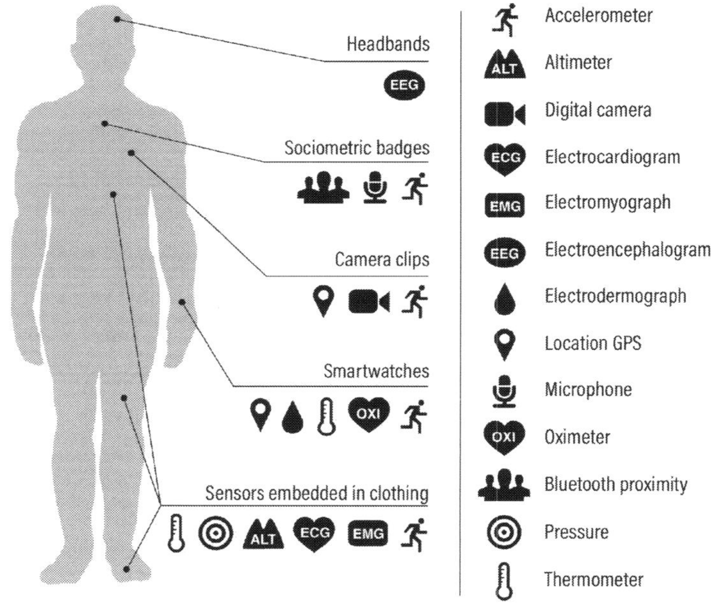

Source: Piwek et al, PLOS Medicine (2016) 13(2) e1001953; February 2, 2016.

Digital therapeutics (DTx) lead to earlier intervention and prevent late-stage complications

M-health not only empowers patients in terms of sensoring body movements, therefore enhancing diagnostics, but it also can be harnessed as a therapeutic tool in the form of digital therapeutics, or DTx. Both the m-health and DTx markets are among the most vibrant ecosystems in the overall health care industry. Despite the global economic slowdown due to COVID-19 (and probably also because of it), DTx, m-health and the overall digital technology space remained one of the fastest-growing sectors in the entire health care industry, with a record year-over-year forty-five percent jump in 2020 and global funding of $26.5 billion.[109] Given this resilience in the face of global adversity, it is one of the most attractive sectors for investors to date. The global digital health market was valued at $116 billion in 2019 and is expected to hit around $833 billion by 2027, with a compound annual growth rate (CAGR) of 27.9% from 2020 to 2027.[141]

From a policymaker perspective, the US FDA has acknowledged the crucial importance of the digital momentum, and its role along the health continuum, by creating the Digital Health Center of Excellence (DHCE). "[This] *marks the next stage in applying a comprehensive approach to digital health technology to realize its full potential to empower consumers to make better-informed decisions about their own health and provide new options for facilitating prevention, early diagnosis of life-threatening diseases, and management of chronic conditions outside of traditional care settings,"* former FDA commissioner Dr Stephen Hahn said in a statement.[142]

Between 2016 and 2020, the FDA approved sixty-four AI/ML-based medical devices and algorithms for diagnosing, managing and treating a wide variety of medical conditions. Of these, twenty-nine were publicly mentioned in FDA press releases.[143] (See figure 4.4.) So, in addition to telehealth, which fosters connectivity, DTx complements the therapeutic armamentarium, and greatly enhances patient self-management and wellbeing. DTx is not, and will not, replace conventional therapies. Rather, it complements care and research, primarily because of its integral functionality to serve with patient self-management and reporting of symptoms and PROMs to providers.

Altogether, they represent a solid addition that leads to personalized medicine while also significantly lowering costs for the patient and the system.

Particularly, the mental component of healthy living continues to gain attention. For example, novel sensor technologies can capture and measure steps and gait patterns for patients with Parkinson's disease, muscle dystrophy or multiple sclerosis.[144,145] Transmission of data is in real time, and patient and providers can directly interact through an open-channel platform. Availability is twenty-four hours a day, seven days a week, and not restrained to opening hours at the clinic or doctor's office. Global funding for companies operating in the mental health space, applying technology to psychological, emotional or social wellbeing, surged to over $2 trillion over the course of 2020.[109] This has certainly been fueled by the social distancing and isolation that people experienced throughout the pandemic that year. Also in 2020, the FDA rapidly approved the first video game as a proven therapeutic intervention for patients suffering from ADHD (attention-deficit/hyperactivity disorder).[146]

One of the first examples of a DTx as an integrated user platform is the Sleepio app for sleep disorders. It is unique in the sense that it is a clinically proven device that combines clinical and social determinants of health. Within the world's first randomized study for digital sleep intervention, as per the manufacturer's website,

Sleepio has shown to be significantly more effective than a placebo, not only in reducing physical symptoms such as high blood pressure, but also in helping patients improve their daytime activities and work effectiveness.[147-150]

Policy enabling DTx approvals is a prime example of what is feasible when governmental will meets health expert knowledge.

Another impressive example is the fast progress that the Merkel administration has made in Germany via an unprecedented public-private multi-stakeholder collaboration, which led to the passing of a new Digital Healthcare Act in record time at the end of 2019.[151] Within a year of that, ten prescribable applications, known as DIGAs, were created based on a fast-tracked approval process. Figure 4.5 provides a brief overview of these DIGAs at the time of writing this book. Their product functionalities cover detection, monitoring, treatment and palliation of diseases, as well as symptom control in the case of disabilities.

The German government soon followed by preparing an additional law, set to further surpass expectations in terms of speed and innovation of modernizing care. Based on the master digital health law and its prescription apps, the Digital Care Applications (known as DIPAs, or digitale Pflegeanwendungen) hold the promise of enhancing home care for patients with reduced mobility and special needs.[152] Overall, the German D-Health ecosystem is one of the fastest-growing markets today, and thus a role model for many other countries in terms of solutions, access and multi-party cooperation.

In summary, one of the remaining challenges that developers, clinicians and researchers will need to figure out soon is how to deal with the increasing number of people suffering from multiple illnesses at the same time; *co-morbidities* in medical language. We will see the full potential of technology once a single patient can manage multiple conditions in one app, such as monitoring blood sugar, blood pressure, gait and sleep in the case of a patient with diabetes, hypertension, Parkinson's disease and insomnia. Essentially, D-Health brings more equality to health care. People have the same access to information and care plans as providers, and can embrace the care for themselves.

Figure 4.4. FDA-approved AI/ML devices and D-Health technologies.

NAME	INDICATION
AI ECG Platform	ECG analysis
AI-Rad Companion	CT imaging – pulmonary
AI-Rad Companion	CT imaging – cardiovascular
AiCE	Noise reduction
Arterys Cardio DL	Cardiovascular imaging
Arterys Oncology DL	Diagnostic
Arterys MICA	Liver, lung imaging
Accipiolx	Stroke triage
BriefCase	Patient triage
ContaCT	Stroke detection imaging
cmTriage	Mammogram workflow
Critical Care Suite	Chest x-ray pneumothorax
Deep Learning	Image reconstruction
DreaMed	Type I diabetes management
EchoMD Automated	Ejection fraction analysis

EchoGo Core	Cardiovascular function report
Eko Analysis	Cardiac monitor
EnsoSleep	Diagnostic of sleep disorders
FerriSmart	Liver iron concentration
Guardian Connect	Blood glucose changes
HealthPNX	Chest x-ray interpretation
icobrain	MRI brain interpretation
Idx Detection	Diabetic retinopathy
ProFound AI	Mammography
QuantX	Cancer detection imaging
OsteoDetect	Wrist fracture imaging
SubtleMR (x2)	Image processing
TranparaTM	Mammogram workflow

Source: Adapted from Benjamens et al[143]

Figure 4.5. DIGAs approved in Germany.

DIGA NAME	INDICATION
Elevida	Multiple sclerosis
Invirto	Agoraphoby, panic attacks, social phobias
Kalmeda	Tinnitus
M-sense migräne	Migraine
Rehappy	Cerebral ischemia, cerebral bleeding
Selfapy	Depression
Somnio	Insomnia
Velibra	Agoraphoby, panic attacks, social phobias
Vivira	Arthrosis
Zanadio	Obesity

Source: www.bfarm.de [151]

Software technology improves adherence to medication

Common sense tells us that medicines don't work if you don't take them. However, it is a frequently overlooked clinical and economic reality. Twenty years ago, the WHO issued a seminal publication aimed at enhancing collaborative efforts to increase adherence to medications, reporting of side effects, and overall pharmacovigilance reporting in order to improve health.[153] Although antidiabetic, antihypertensive and anti-cholesterol treatments have well proven their effectiveness in large clinical studies, in reality it is also well documented that fifty percent of patients (or up to eighty percent according to some sources) don't take their pills regularly, stop them early, or never start taking them at all.[154]

With more and more people carrying wearables and devices, D-Health is potentially a promising way to impact patient outcomes by increasing education and self-empowerment, and changing patients' behavior so that they are actually willing to adhere to their medication regimens.[155] To take it further, there are multiple initiatives investigating how to include patients in a novel incentive system that rewards them for better results when pre-defined outcomes are met (refer to VBHC in chapter three).

Utilizing this approach of behavioral and reward mechanisms to ensure adherence, the team at Collabree, through their ongoing clinical trial entitled 'An Intervention to Improve the Regularity of Medication Intake', hypothesizes that financial incentives improve motivation and self-empowerment, and therefore strengthen medication adherence for patients with hypertension in an ambulatory setting.[156,157]

"Increasing the effectiveness of adherence interventions may have a far greater impact on the health of the population than any improvement in specific medical treatments." [153]

Adherence is both a personal and a system matter.

Failing to take a prescribed therapy leads to poor disease control and lowers the chances of better health outcomes for the patient. At the same time, it leads to an increased burden and cost for countries and their health care systems. To illustrate the extent that the problem can take, see the story my grandmother used to tell me "The old lady wants to live" in breakout box 3.

In the US, medication non-adherence leads to premature deaths and to an increased use of health care services. Between $100 billion and $300 billion of avoidable health care costs, and approximately 125,000 deaths, have been attributed to non-adherence per year in the US.[158,159] Looking at Europe, it is estimated that non-adherence contributes to nearly 200,000 premature deaths per year and costs European governments €125 billion annually in excess health care services.[160] In Switzerland alone, Santésuisse estimates a saving potential of more than three billion Swiss francs, if only 100,000 of the two million people with chronic conditions in Switzerland improved their adherence.[161]

In summary, thousands of lives – and billions of dollars, euros or Swiss francs – could be spared if better patient education and self-management accompanied the automatic refill of prescription pills.

BREAKOUT BOX 3: THE OLD LADY WANTS TO LIVE

"But I also want to live!" sighed the old lady at her doctor.

The doctor was scratching his head. The lady seemed to be doing perfectly fine, but her blood pressure levels were far too high for her age. He would see health problems arise for her soon.

So he said, "I don't understand. I have been prescribing these new pills to you for six months now. Every other patient I have given these to has seen an improvement. But not you. I'm wondering what's going on. Have you actually been taking them?"

She replied, "Of course not! I took your prescription to the pharmacy every month, went home and then flushed them down the toilet. At last, you want to live, the pharmacist wants to live, and I want to live, too!"

THE TIME IS RIPE FOR SMART POLICYMAKERS

Personally, what I find most inspiring about the digital revolution in health care is the important role of the policymaker.

Value creation and assessment is increasingly data-driven, and advanced analytics is the key enabler. Capturing patient data, sharing data across stakeholders, and turning data into value-adding solutions for the patient is the true revolution of digital in health care. Since everything is instant and immediately available to everyone who needs the information, the field is advancing at an unprecedented speed. At this pace, we cannot anticipate what the next round of innovation will bring. Who expected that we would live by mobile devices twenty years ago? Similar trends can be seen in cellphone use. At the start of the 2000s, there were 740 million cellphone subscriptions worldwide. Two decades later, that number has surpassed eight billion, meaning there are now more cellphones in the world than people.[162] Likewise, in health care, digital applications to treat and prevent diseases have never existed before, and regulatory frameworks need to be adapted to ensure their safe and effective use.

But this is not the policymakers' and the health authorities' responsibility alone. As I described earlier, we all need to fundamentally shift our mindset on how we engage with the policymaker. The worst-case scenario would be for an inventor to approach the FDA, after years of development and user testing, only to hear, *"No, we can't approve this new AI-powered device because we don't have a regulation box into which this new tech invention fits."*

Today, the world of D-Health does not always fit into the traditional set of regulatory boxes. Tomorrow, there is a unique opportunity for software developers to proactively engage with policymakers and co-create new regulations together, in parallel with developing new digital solutions, which saves time and money, and ultimately benefits patients.

Without going into too much detail, there are some macro-level geographic differences between the regulatory environments for go-to-market strategies. For example, in the US, the strategy is fast, consumer-focused, and geared toward B2C solutions targeting behavioral and lifestyle aspects. Additionally, there is a free economy of selling and purchasing health datasets. It allows for fast prototyping of new apps and incorporating consumer insights during the development stages, and therefore ensures more mature final soft- and hardware for a later therapeutic solution that needs to be FDA approved. In Europe, the focus is leaning toward data privacy and the emphasis of clinically proven interventions following the standard drug development processes (see chapter one, figure 1.6). This means it takes somewhat longer before a digital solution gets to the patient in Europe, but it delivers more therapeutically focused solutions than in a traditional B2B fashion.

Different countries are in various stages of digitalization and reforming their policies in light of the D-Health revolution. In the following section, I will highlight a few regions and countries, and provide some additional clarifications around electronic data terminology, needs for interoperability, and data privacy.

It all starts with electronic data capture
The central lever to enable smart health care is the digitization of data at the point of care: at the patient and at the provider.

There is no digital development and no digital solution without digital data. You can't feed a computer with paper notes. It needs to be fed with electronic data and it needs a program that analyzes these data. Otherwise, the whole investment is useless. And, VBHC and DTx will remain parts of a dream, not a reality. It is like a pair of knitting needles – you can't work on that pullover to keep you warm if you don't have the wool or the needles to knit it.

So, establishing new IT infrastructure, software platforms, standardization of data capture, and regulatory frameworks that enable as well as govern the collection of personal patient data, is a herculean endeavor. And it is foremost a collaborative effort. The software developer can't do it alone. The provider can't do it alone. The policymaker and the regulator can't do it alone. We have seen in chapter two what the first generation of EMR development has created in terms of catastrophic burden and cost to doctors, nurses and hospital administrators if done and developed in isolation.

The ultimate beneficiary of a digitally integrated system of health is the patient. Empowered to own their own data, patients play a crucial role to steer the care delivery chain into a novel era.

Figure 4.6 depicts the main target audiences and objectives of the three forms of electronic patient data capture: EMR (electronic medical record), EHR (electronic health record) and EPR (electronic patient record). These acronyms, and their variations in different languages, are being used quite interchangeably. For the sake of simplicity, I will continue to use EHR.

In summary, as a one-stop-shop solution, EHR is dependent on a collaborative and transparent effort, with data entry, maintenance and analytics being a shared responsibility. Doctors, nurses, pharmacists and insurers operate at a high degree of cooperation to make such a model a success. Furthermore, data capture needs to be standardized. Otherwise, there is a risk of incompatibility and therefore continued wastage in the system.

Figure 4.6. Various platform solutions for electronic health data capture.

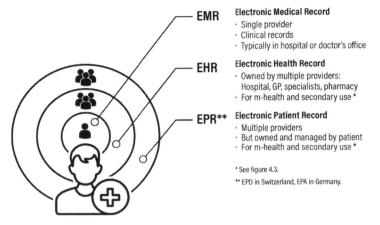

EMR — Electronic Medical Record
· Single provider
· Clinical records
· Typically in hospital or doctor's office

EHR — Electronic Health Record
· Owned by multiple providers:
  Hospital, GP, specialists, pharmacy
· For m-health and secondary use *

EPR** — Electronic Patient Record
· Multiple providers
· But owned and managed by patient
· For m-health and secondary use *

* See figure 4.3.
** EPD in Switzerland, EPA in Germany.

(Note: the further from the center, the more users, and the more interoperable the power of the platform becomes.)

Interoperability of EHR is the key to eradicate fragmentation and redundancies

Today, health professionals have no holistic access to all patient data end to end. Similarly, patients are deprived of better care because doctors are not equipped with the right tools to comprehensively share data from one provider to another, from patient to provider, or from pharmacy to provider. This fragmentation is not only a nuisance for the patient or the doctor experience, but it is the primary cause of wasteful care delivery and uncontrolled cost explosion. Generally referred to as 'interoperability', this cross-system communication has to be improved and expanded, and silos broken down.

There are two main barriers to full interoperability of systems: cost and data privacy. It is not about the technical solutions or the lack of innovative software; there is plenty. What gets in the way is a disconnected ecosystem and the lack of available resources to transform the infrastructures.

Firstly, in terms of cost and investments, this is where governments play a critical role in addition to providing the required regulatory framework. In order to keep the lights on, there are times when analog and digital have to co-exist in parallel. This comes with short-term extra costs, human and financial, until new resources become available from the shutdown of analog systems. Such as in the example of the UK D-Health strategy, where the UK government is providing £16 million in funding to hospitals across England to introduce EHR and digital prescribing.[163] Supporting hospitals, doctors, payers and other actors to effectively transition through this temporary cost bottleneck takes time. Therefore, it is not rare for the development of sustainable digital solutions to span years or even decades.

We need to find the right balance. 100% data privacy won't work. 100% data transparency won't work either.

Secondly, the handling of patient data has to comply with the most rigorous moral standards and ethics. What we can observe in the debate around data protection is that various countries and societies set different bars and thresholds. There is little that is easily transferrable from one to another. However, there are some common principles that can be considered. There is a French saying, "You can't hold the money for the butter and the butter at the same time." It refers to the fact that full and waterproof anonymization of data will never be possible. Particularly not if we say we want to foster more transparency and data sharing. Does technology hold the means to "bake in" privacy by default? At least, the field of cybersecurity, blockchain and patient privacy intelligence is booming, evolving into an attractive tech sector on its own. In 2020 alone, a global funding spike of over $4 trillion marked a record year in terms of cybertechnology market expansion.[109]

Isn't it strange to see that all the tracing apps for COVID-19 didn't show the desired outcome in the Western world because of privacy issues? Our credit card companies have all the info they need, but a health app designed to stop people from dying fails to succeed due to our concerns around sharing our whereabouts. By the way, smartwatches are collecting tons of health data, which most certainly are sold to interested parties. These paradoxes need regulations, not to prohibit but to improve health outcomes. Who can be against this? To this point, Philippe van Holle, when he was writing the foreword to this book, said, *"This book beautifully showcases how digitalization can catalyze public-private initiatives, bridge solutions between data protection and data transparency, and find ways for patients to become digitally empowered to steer their own health."*

Overall, the trend is promising, with most countries realizing that the lack of digital is similarly or more dangerous than the lack of waterproof data privacy. A handful of countries are showing how electronic data capture – from a citizen, patient and government perspective – is feasible and can be done quite successfully.

Roll-out of digital in health care in select countries

As we have seen through the German and US AI/ML and DTx examples, electronic transformation is becoming a reality at full speed. You may wonder which country is most advanced and has the most digitalized health care system. There is no one answer, as the task is complex and the acceleration has only really just begun. However, there are some countries that stand out.

Denmark

One country that has set an example on data interoperability is Denmark, with the implementation of its Data Analytics Center (DAC) in 2020.[164] Its vision is to overcome data silos across the public and private sectors to enhance the development of, and access to, safe new medicines and devices. The DAC provides a fully interoperable supercomputer platform to connect real-world data, industry patient-level data and pharmacovigilance data utilizing advanced analytics in a safe cloud environment.[165] This could only be achieved based on a long-standing tradition of electronic data capture. Nearly all GPs use EHR to exchange records (ninety-eight percent), to receive lab results (100 percent), and to send referrals to hospitals (ninety-seven percent).[166] *"In epidemiological terms, the population of Denmark is an open cohort with known dates of entry and exit, and with various types of rich health data recorded between those dates."* A moment of spotlight onto the DAC has been the unfolding of the COVID-19 pandemic. Data from COVID-19 patients in various stages of clinical symptomology were measured, processed and analyzed in real time. This instant data capture allowed the DAC to generate insights on early intervention and optimal patient management. Learnings could be redeployed directly to new patients at the same pace that the data were collected.[167]

Estonia

Ranked number one in the digital health index of smart health systems worldwide, Estonia has grown into a fully interoperable society, with over ninety-nine percent of its government, services and health care being online.[168] With its unique citizen identifier, it has been a global role model for over thirty years around the successful adoption of e-services by its civic society, and the safe use of patient health data in both the public and private spaces. *"Estonia has led to creating a society with more transparency, trust and efficiency. We have learned that developing e-solutions is not merely about adding something (a digital layer) but changing everything."*[169] If you're interested, it's worth checking out the e-Estonia platform, which provides training, seminars and online tools to inform the transformation with regard to e-health and cybersecurity possibilities.[169]

The European Union

The EU has long prioritized investment into interoperable infrastructure throughout Europe. The European Commission's Directorate-General for Communications Networks, Content and Technology (DG CNECT) is responsible for developing a single digital market to generate smart, sustainable and inclusive growth in Europe.[170] In conjunction with the Directorate-General for Health and Food Safety (DG SANTE), the main health care strategy revolves around three priorities: enabling easier citizen access to health data; stimulating innovation to foster sharing of big data on the way to personalized medicine along the health continuum (prevention to treatment); and tailoring investments into health dashboard infrastructures, with the aim of fostering integrated, multi-disciplinary care teams and home-based care delivery.[171] As with so many international, national and local initiatives in

D-Health, many of these have been kept on the slow burner and only really gained momentum in the wake of the COVID-19 pandemic. EU4Health, the new EU health program, has been funded with €5.1 billion to increase the resilience of health systems, and to help ensure the EU applies research results and supports the translation of health innovation into clinical practice.[172] Digital transformation in the health care sector is also an integral part of the recently released EU Pharmaceutical Strategy 2025.[173]

The UK

The UK and Germany together account for eighty percent of the European digital VC market.[174] The NHS has recently hit a major milestone in transforming its system of health: in the largest known public data network transition, it has successfully migrated from its legacy N3 platform to the new Health and Social Care Network (HSCN). It is estimated that this disruptive change from analog to digital will save £75 million per year, and give organizations faster access to data at reduced cost.[175] Notably, this initiative showcases two outstanding facts. Firstly, the power of the policymaker in taking bold decisions, and making upfront investments that ensure economic gains for all stakeholders later down the road. Secondly, it is an alliance between public and private organizations (that are members of the NHS) that collaboratively made this transition a reality. Patrick Clark, HSCN Programme Director at NHS Digital, said, *"This is a hugely significant achievement both in terms of the scale and the benefit of what has been delivered. Reforming long-standing services in order to promote real choice, competition, innovation and value for money is always difficult but the HSCN initiative demonstrates what can be achieved when you work collaboratively across the health and care system, and industry."*

The role of the policymaker, and the role of novel partnerships between providers, academia, pharma and payer in particular, is crucial to make this digital transformation a success.

MAKING THE DIGITAL TRANSFORMATION IN HEALTH CARE A SUCCESS

The future of health care will be personal.

AI/ML and D-Health will massively disrupt traditional ways of delivering care by putting the patient's health continuum at the center and empowering people to manage their own health.

Yes, health care is late to the Fourth Industrial Revolution, but the pace at which it is catching up is mind-boggling. Both public and private actors started working hand-in glove, and are deploying massive investments. The number of start-up companies in the realm of m-health and AI is booming. And it is fascinating to see how governments and policymakers are jumping on the band-wagon of digitalization.

Adoption of smart digital solutions in health care is contingent on building a strong basis of trust, which comes through early involvement of all relevant actors and civic society.

In order to avoid mistakes of the past (and avoid wasting money we don't have on tools we don't need) time invested collaboratively at the earliest development stages is time well spent for adoption later on and should be more important than speed-to-market. The bad experiences with the first generation EMRs go deep with doctors and nurses. Hence, proactively communicating with transparency, investing in education and showcasing the benefits of novel AI/ML and D-Health solutions will alleviate the hesitation felt by many health professionals and by civic society.[176-178]

The bar sits high, as the level of IT infrastructure and digital maturity is globally still very low. For example, in Germany the excitement is high and changes are real with the before mentioned DIGA implementation, and a recent survey has shown eight out of ten doctors are enthusiastic at the prospect of tomorrow's significant workload reductions.[179] However, today's reality is still analog. Almost all doctors (ninety-three percent) in the same survey still communicate on paper, with less than half of hospitals (forty-four percent) using any electronic data capture system.

Digital breaks down silos in health care. By compressing time and space, it brings back the gift of time between the main stakeholders: patients, providers, pharma, payers and policymakers.

By acquiring digital health literacy, an updated digitized infrastructure, and the interoperability of IT systems, we will deepen the interconnectivity of all stakeholders in the ecosystem, empowering self-management for patients and driving efficiencies for the system. In short, digital is not merely a dream. It fills the stage with trust and is the technical enabler for the smart orchestration of a *Tango for Five*, as we will see in the following and final chapter.

TOP TAKEAWAYS FROM CHAPTER FOUR

☑ Digital on its own is not the Holy Grail in health care. But when it serves a well-defined purpose, and when it is co-created with all the right actors around the table, it holds the promise to radically modernize our systems and make health care smarter, faster and more efficient.

☑ In order to reap the full transformational potential of AI/ML and D-Health, investments in education by the public and private sectors must become a priority in order to rapidly improve the digital literacy of medical staff and patients, and therefore drive trust and adoption.

☑ Smart policymakers and regulators who have good insights into technology, and are able to co-create pathways for approvals and use these together with software developers, hold the key to progress. Life sciences, pharma and policy should adopt a smart mindset shift toward increased collaboration and proactive strategic engagement. The following chapter outlines a collaborative playbook to orchestrate such a smart *Tango for Five*.

CHAPTER 5

Adopting a playbook for multi-party collaboration to catalyze change behavior

"We build too many walls and not enough bridges."

~ ISAAC NEWTON

BRINGING IN THE OTHER VIEW

If collaborating is the new winning proposition and partnerships are the new North Star in health care, then how do we reconcile this vision with today's reality?

As I was reflecting on this, I came across a webinar featuring Timothy Shriver, the bestselling author of *Fully Alive: Discovering What Matters Most*. At the opening of his lecture, he included a quote from a Martin Luther King Jr sermon titled "Loving your Enemies", which King delivered in 1957:

"Darkness cannot drive out darkness. Only light can do that. Hate cannot drive out hate.Only love can do that." [180]

So often in my career, I have encountered dead-ends and insurmountable barriers to collaboration that felt like darkness. Over and over again, I have experienced situations where great ideas have struggled to gain momentum due to differences of personal opinion on the road to implementation. (I'm sure you have, too.)

I have also witnessed many times how individual leaders, acting as integrators and mediators, were able to drive resolution by bringing light back into a room of conflict, and doing so in a collaborative, empathetic manner.

So to put this into practice, I encourage you to complete this exercise, shared by Tim Shriver in his lecture.

"I invite you to bring to mind one situation over the past days or week where you personally experienced a moment that you or someone else brought light into a situation of darkness."

Be it in your personal life – with your spouse, your children, your friends – or in the workplace, picture a situation where, despite adversity and conflict, someone made an unsolicited step toward the other, presumably offended person.

Pause for a couple of minutes and reflect on how this experience makes you feel.

With this exercise, Tim reminds us how easy and simple it can be to work on our empathy muscle. It unleashes energy when we see beyond the fence and start stepping into the shoes of the other person. Seeing a situation not only through our own lens, but through the lens of the other person.

Taking another perspective helps to dissociate the problem from the person.

Talking about large-scale political matters that are plaguing our societies at the dawn of this new millennium, Tim says, *"We lost the sense for relationships with shared meaning."*

Bang.

As I'm listening to him, I am thinking, "How true this is in health care, too. This brings it straight to the point."

As human beings, our instincts regularly hold us hostage, as we often make snap assumptions. We judge the person in front of us by the picture or statement they are making. We live by opposing binary views, thinking our view is right, instead of taking a step back, pausing and reflecting on a different view, and giving credit to the other view. Or asking ourselves a simple question: how would the problem be seen by a third person?

Removing ourselves from the immediate problem, and taking a step back to see the greater whole, is what we can choose to do to start recognizing the other view ourselves.

GROWING THE COLLECTIVE VALUE PIE

The quandary of health care is that our scientific innovations are infinite while our resources to afford those innovations are limited. Instinctively, in a world driven by competition for resources, we seem to apply this concept of "fixed resources" to solution finding whenever we come to the negotiation table. One of the most destructive assumptions for any negotiator – but especially in health care – is to believe that we have a "fixed pie" of resources. As described in previous chapters, we do not have an issue of resource shortages in health care, but an issue of resources in the wrong place in a system that rewards the wrong incentives. What we need is leaders who ask a different ingoing question, such as:

"What outcomes do I wish to generate for patients and my stakeholders, and with whom do I need to cooperate to get to these results?"

This is what will generate value and grow the collective value pie. The Program on Negotiation (PON) at Harvard University states, *"The mythical fixed-pie mindset leads us to interpret the most competitive situations as purely win-lose."*[181]

Value creation requires an active effort and the will to collaborate. The Cambridge Dictionary defines collaboration as *"the situation of two or more people working together to create or achieve the same thing."*

As we have seen in previous chapters, the traditional FFS model has favored a silo-type mentality leading to mostly transactional, binary and short-term engagements. The issue, though, is that working in silos doesn't lead to creating the same thing, and hence doesn't create value. For no one. Stockpiling benefits by one actor in just their part of the health care pie, and shifting cost to the other parts of the pie, actually destroys value. By focusing on short-term transactions, we are missing out on the opportunities to leverage long-term synergies.

Because health care is so complex and diverse, none of the actors will ever have all the required expertise, knowledge and experience to solve the problem of our broken health care systems alone. Each of the constituents has their own culture, language and ways of working. Often, these practicalities get in the way and blur the view of the common goal. This can be detrimental to progress, because the solutions to our problems as health care leaders often lie outside of our own expertise.

Assuming everyone wants the best for the patient, how can we leverage this shared purpose to break down silos and reconnect the dots? As a highly interactive and interdisciplinary activity, co-creating solutions together requires everyone to recenter their thinking and actions around the right mindset (see chapter one, figure 1.9). In today's highly interconnected world, every actor has a role to play – including government, life sciences, doctors, insurers and patients. All experts need to work hand-in-glove from day one to get the mutual value-gain solutions right. This includes researchers in the lab and in the clinics, leaders in academia and in pharmaceuticals, regulatory agencies and reimbursement author-ities. We cannot afford to waste time or money on this path.

Hence, there is an urgency to overcome legal, policy and economic barriers to achieve collaboration.

The only way to achieve this in a hypercomplex
health care ecosystem is by adopting a collaborative
approach and by forging novel partnerships.

COVID-19 has shown how fast barriers can be broken down.

Other public-private partnerships (PPPs), described in chapter two, and a plethora of smaller projects in the realm of VBHC and digital, described in chapters three and four, demonstrate that this is feasible in health care, nevertheless. What we need to do is spread the word, share best practice, and learn from those successful examples.

Vanessa Candeias is a prominent global health care leader, spearheading PPPs on national governmental and international institution levels. Having worked with the WHO, as the health care leader at the WEF, and now as a leader for The Hepatitis Fund (which aims to end hepatitis by 2030), she has unique views about what it takes to be successful in growing the collective value pie through collaboration. In my podcast series #LetsTalkValue, she nicely summarizes a survey that she conducted with over 120 leaders who have been actively engaged in PPPs. This includes leaders from the public sector, private sector and civic society, as well as academic experts.[182] *"Verena, out of the five factors that people across the public and private* [sectors] *consistently report as bottlenecks, the number one barrier to collaboration is mistrust,"* she tells me. It is *the* underlying theme that drives the other four factors people bring to the negotiation table: a worry about conflict of interest, a lack of leadership, a lack of transparency amid concerns of a "hidden" agenda, and cultural and/or organizational differences.[183]

Before I move on to explore which tools we can deploy to overcome these bottlenecks, let me pause for a moment to share a brief thought on the term "negotiation".

For some, "negotiation" may read as "conflict". Then, you may think, "But I don't really have a conflict. I just need to get that project done and remove that obstacle with these other people." For others, talking about negotiation in health care may make them think of pricing negotiations or legal disputes. William Ury and the late Roger Fisher, founders of the Harvard Negotiation Project (HNP) and authors of the seminal book on negotiation *Getting to Yes*, described it as, *"back-and-forth communication designed to reach an agreement when you and the other side have some interests that are shared and others that are opposed."*[184,185]

*As a matter of fact, conflict or no conflict,
we are negotiating all the time.*

With our children, our spouse, and while speaking to the cashier about the validity of that discount voucher. Negotiation is part of our daily living without us necessarily being conscious of it. Truth be told, we are negotiating with ourselves all day long, too. Do I go to that fitness class today or do I cancel it and meet up with my friend instead? For the purpose of this book, I occasionally use the term "negotiation" interchangeably when describing the process of collaboration between the various health care leaders.

Figure 5.2. Boom: the world, similar or different?

PARTISAN PERCEPTIONS

Remaining fixed in our own views, without taking on a different perspective, is what we generally refer to as "partisan perceptions". Coming to the negotiation table with pre-conceived ideas and perceptions makes it harder to work through the essence of why we came to the table in the first place. It creates the unfortunate ground to believe the other person is actually *wrong*. This in turn can nurture mistrust when the other person feels attacked, misunderstood and disrespected. Furthermore, this kind of judgmental "inner-talk" with ourselves makes us forget the common goal of why we want to work together. It makes us see more differences than commonalities.

As depicted in figure 5.1, you may realize how awkward it feels when two people look at exactly the same thing but have completely different interpretations of what they see. As illustrated in figure 5.2, people tend to report the differences and rarely the commonalities, yet it is the same reality.

Figure 5.1. Partisan perceptions: rabbit or duck?

Source: Jastrow, J. (1899). The mind's eye. *Popular Science Monthly*, 54, 299-312.

As alluded to earlier, in health care we are full of partisan perceptions that are deeply anchored within the silos of providers, pharma, payers, policy and also patients. The fundamental problem here being that opinions, positions and silos undermine innovation and value.

Why?

Because partisan perceptions trigger a behavior of bargaining. Since you can only see one view, you remain stuck to that one opinion and you negotiate around defending your position. It shuts down the blinds on creating new solutions that lie outside of your ingoing opinion, and that would require hearing and observing other views.

In many countries, the culture of haggling and bargaining back and forth on price in markets and bazaars is deeply ingrained in society. It can work well in private environments with friends and family, too. It is easy and quick, and helps people agree on which dinner to prepare, which restaurant to choose, and which new bike to buy for their child. However, when the stakes are high, more money is on the table and more people are involved, the risk of someone losing out and, overall, reaching a suboptimal agreement, is high.

What is the main reason for this?

It is much harder to overcome and concede on a position than on a principle.

You cannot fix the problem with the same tools that created it. Hanging on to old ways of working, by finger-pointing and singling out villains, won't solve the quandary in health care.

What we need is a complete mindset shift that moves us beyond positions and that enables us to see the person behind the problem. Adopting a set of principles that help us to actually disentangle the problem from the person. It is by formulating our perspectives as options, and listening to other perspectives with interest, that we will find the key to unlocking the positional graveyard of innovation.

We all came to health care for a reason: to care for patients and create value for the system. Either with a passion for the patient, a passion for science, or an entrepreneurial spirit to contribute to new health solutions. What unites all of us is a strong, genuine sense of purpose. Isn't this an excellent starting block to explore a playbook that can effectively orchestrate a mutual-gain *Tango for Five*?

THE SEVEN STEPS

Remember the tango coach for leadership, Pablo Pugliese, whom I referred to in the introduction of this book? Here is where his common vocabulary for a common dance comes into play. Learning to collaborate in health care is like learning how to dance a tango for two or, in this case, for five – the steps are the same.

Things are relatively easy when two parties are involved. However, co-creating solutions with many parties at the table is really hard.

But the good news is: it can be done. It has been done and it becomes easier with practice.

One possible way forward is to pull from a blueprint that has long proven its worth.

"Unfortunately, most people are not natural-born negotiators. The good news is that research consistently shows that most people can significantly improve their negotiation skills through education, preparation, and practice."[186]

I already mentioned the late Roger Fisher at the HNP, who spear-headed much of this pragmatic playbook, summarized within a set of seven principles, that has led to conflict resolution in a wide array of complex situations since its inception half a century ago.

As outlined in figure 5.3, these steps represent a powerful frame-work to mutually grow the value pie whenever two or more parties are collaborating toward a common goal. Once a common purpose is clearly set, it can be successfully applied in large-scale negoti-ations, such as the breakdown of apartheid in South Africa in 1991, the Camp David Accords in 1978, and the resolution of the US-Ira-nian hostage crisis in 1979. As a result, it has evolved into the gold standard for conflict resolution in business and legal media-tion.[187,188] Today, it is among the top-ranked negotiation frameworks taught in many business schools around the world.[184,188-190]

Figure 5.3. Seven steps to successfully coordinate multi-party collaborations in a *Tango for Five*.

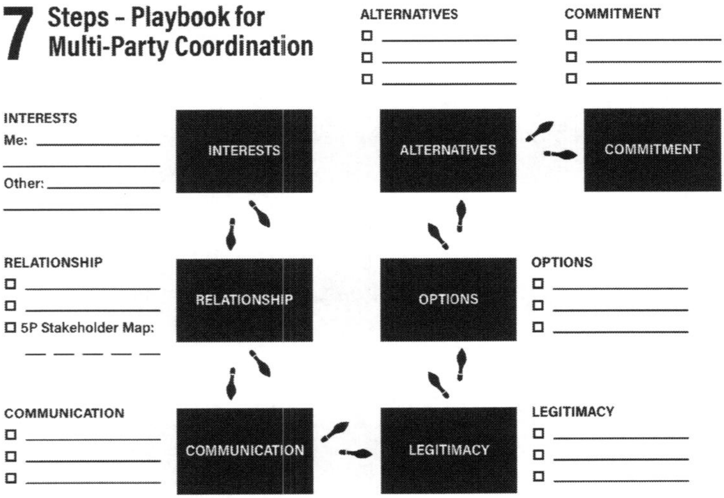

There really is no reason why such a framework could not be successful in helping to solve the competing interests and complexities in health care. We don't have a lack of solutions in health care. We have a lack of the right mindset and skillset to enable leaders to bring those solutions to fruition. I was fortunate enough to be introduced to this playbook over a decade ago and, together with many talented colleagues in health care, have been able to witness its power to open doors that were thought to be sealed for good.

Just like in the tango, the playbook of seven steps can be seen as a common vocabulary to orchestrate the cooperation between health care leaders.

Although the playbook is depicted sequentially in figure 5.3, there really isn't a particular process, rule or order to the seven steps. The way I listed them is only for the sake of clarity and simplicity. Just like in a tango, as Pablo reminds us, leaders who use a common vocabulary can create space to co-create innovative new solutions together. Additionally, the blueprint in this figure can serve as a preparation guide to any important meeting or negotiation. Also, the trio of questions listed after each step may help you in the planning phases of critical negotiations, conversations and meetings.

So, without further ado, let's learn the seven steps of the tango dance playbook.

Interests

For a successful collaboration, it is best not to come to the table with prejudices about the other person, team or problem. Instead, it's better to focus on getting to know the other person, by listening to their objectives and needs, and seeking to understand the obstacles they are facing. This is the most relevant first step to mutual-gain collaboration, followed by formulating your own interests very clearly.

Too often, we fall short on both counts.

Successful negotiation starts with acknowledging and appreciating each other's situations and goals. It does not mean we have to agree and align on all points. In fact, this is unlikely. But it isn't the purpose. It is about drawing an early circle around any common ground and identifying what could possibly be done together. It is about separating the people from the problem and focusing on interests, not positions.

Getting a full perspective on the other party's needs, challenges and interests is what lies at the center of a collaborative strategy. This is where the partisan perceptions of a solo dancer get in our way. They blur the view of what's possible. Consequently, there is little room for imagination on what else is possible outside of our positions. We feel like we're losing face if we "give in" on our position. *"This type of win-lose approach overlooks opportunities to create – and not just distribute – value,"* says Bruce Patten, co-founder of the PON at Harvard University.[191]

Taking a step back and changing the narrative may change the dynamic.

Moving from "I don't like this person" to "I want to get to know this person and their needs" – and asking open-ended questions, demonstrating curiosity and showing empathy – can unfold unprecedented energy. Probing to fully comprehend the situation of the other person, and elaborating on values and vision, is what will trigger similar openness on the other party's side to understand *your* situation and perspectives. Overall, these are the ingredients that set up a long-term focus on the agreement.

Openly sharing mutual interests sets a strong foundation to (re)building trust.

The thing is that people usually don't just walk into a room and start telling you all their interests. Likewise, in the heat of a debate, we ourselves may be strongly committed to "being right" – so much so that we fail to clearly formulate our own situation and objectives. People are usually unaware of their interests and what their true underlying needs are. They are well hidden underneath a layer of opinions and positions. Particularly in the complexity of health care, with strong bargaining powers at the table, things get quickly mixed up with sets of long-standing frustrations, challenges and bad prior experiences. Change fatigue fills the room and drives leaders to believe that nothing has ever changed for the better.

However, carefully listening to whatever people are expressing, especially in their criticism, may give you clues and hints as to what their underlying needs are. If we can refrain from reacting too quickly (perhaps by taking criticism personally) and practice active listening, this may help us to better understand why we came here and what we want to accomplish in the first place.

Moving our narrative from "My opinion is" and "This is wrong!" to "My needs are" and "Help me understand" is a powerful strategy to open up space and time, particularly when several parties are negotiating.

Here are three questions to keep in mind:

- Am I clear on the other parties' needs, challenges and frustrations?
- What does their criticism – if any – tell me about their interests and priorities?
- Am I prepared to clearly articulate my situation, needs and pressures?

Relationships

Teams are made of people. Institutions, companies and hospitals are only as good as their people.

In this day and age of global interconnectedness and value, everything is about relationships and connections between people. It is about investing in relationships with our peer group, and within our organization, company and constituents. It is about building, handling and growing intersectoral relationships. In the twenty-first century, managing complexity in health care effectively means successfully managing interrelationships across a vast variety of stakeholders. The number of permutations is endless: pharma with providers and payers, providers with patients and payers, policy with pharma and providers, and so on. In large webs of networks such as the health care ecosystem, with its interconnected stakeholders, we all need to make a great effort to forge novel partnerships. Given that most of the solutions to our respective problems may actually lie outside of our own functional expertise, and the notion that innovation emerges at the intersection of networks, being able to build bridges with each other holds true transformative potential. It is what will bring value-based health care to reality.

Forging novel partnerships that involve multiple parties is what will make health care of the future successful.

Additionally, value creation means building for the future. The biggest trap of traditional bargaining is that it skews our focus to the short term. We look at the here and now. This is how our reward structure is built: short-term and short-sighted fees for service. There is no incentive to take into account future repercussions of our decisions today. "I want this deal here and now," is our ingoing position more often than not. However, knowing when it is time to negotiate for a better deal, and knowing when it is time to accept the offer before you, is the mark of a skilled negotiator. Having sight of the long-term implications in a relationship is a core principle to build sustainable solutions. A key aspect of this is mastering the art of saying "No". Saving the deal, saving the relationship and still saying "No" is what William Ury outlines in his book, *Getting Past No*, which is a useful reference for anybody who seeks to perfect this rare skill.[192]

*Knowing when to concede on a deal today may be a
good investment in the relationship for the future.*

In health care, we rarely decide on something for the short term
because the impact on patients, systems and infrastructure will
always occur in the future. Solutions will be implemented over
time and their performance will be measured in the future. This
is the nature of value-based health care. It requires long-term
interrelationships of various stakeholders to align on health outcomes, and it takes months and years to capture the value of
these outcomes.

Here are three questions to keep in mind:

- How do I (we) value this relationship in the long run?
- What are the implications of my decisions today for this
  relationship in the future?
- Which are the relevant 5P stakeholders that I can involve
  to add value to the solution?

Communication

*"The success of your negotiation can hinge on your communication
choices, such as whether you threaten or acquiesce, brainstorm jointly
or make firm demands, make silent assumptions about interests or
ask questions to prove them more deeply,"* says the team at PON.[186]

Communicating succinctly about what you are seeking, sharing
openly the pressures you may be under, and explaining what
your limits of authority are, all contribute to provide clarity. It is

a powerful foundation to building credibility and trust. Appreciating the subtleties of vocabulary helps to be very effective in creating an atmosphere conducive to productive outcomes. The importance of expressing views in a non-judgmental way, and linking your intent with curiosity, is the secret sauce of successful negotiators. A simple way to do this is to ask for your counterparts' ideas whenever you feel like saying, "No, but this won't work." Generally referred to as building a "golden bridge", this technique can switch the narrative from "No, but" – and wanting to sell your ideas – to "Yes, I understand, and what about this additional idea?"

Words. Do. Matter.

It comes down to *what* you say and *how* you say things. And what you *don't* say.

Transparency and the nuances of the rhetoric are strong influencers to steer the conversation in a productive direction. Conversely, the wrong word in the wrong context can create unnecessary barriers to agreement. One of the critical skills in multi-party collaborations is being able to differentiate between intent and impact of the words spoken. As mentioned earlier, most of us have grown up in a bargaining culture where we are quick to make snap judgments. One wrong word can have precisely that effect. Watch out for the discrepancy between words and actions. If your goal is increased collaboration and mutual gain, your documents, slide presentations and agreements must be stripped of any "me versus you" and "us versus them" vocabulary. "Me" and "you" should be replaced by a big comprehensive "we", with a focus on delivering solutions together instead of defending our position.

Here are three questions to keep in mind:

- How do I articulate my thoughts? Am I mindful of my communication style, tone and intent?
- Do I contribute to a productive atmosphere, or do I sound threatening or offensive?
- Am I purposeful in my language when using communication channels (emails, phone calls and so on)?

Legitimacy

A sense of fairness is one of the virtues that people value most in negotiations.

People can accept views, opinions and decisions that are different from their own if they are given an explanatory framework on why this is fair to them and others. On the other hand, if people sense they are being taken advantage of, this can fuel snap reactions in a heartbeat. Providing enough benchmarking facts and datapoints helps to prevent a hasty turn in the conversation. *"To succeed in negotiation, we need to put forth proposals that others will view as legitimate and fair."*[186] As it turns out, legitimacy is one of the strongest differentiators between a positional bargaining strategy and a mutual-gain strategy. It is the key that unlocks partisan perceptions.

Building relationships based on facts and legitimacy builds trust and focuses the conversation on the purpose rather than on positions.

Focusing on legitimacy can transform a transactional sell into a sustainable solution. It is tempting to think about collaboration as a way of reaching a good compromise. What we tend to mean by this is to meet somewhere in the middle and believe that this is the best reachable agreement for both sides.

Unfortunately, good compromise is the enemy of growing value through great solutions.

Picture this for a minute: you are in a flea market trying to purchase a unique vinyl disc of Pink Floyd's *The Wall.* Since it's such a unique piece, the seller puts forward a $100 price tag, but you really only have $20 to spend. In a typical bargaining fashion, you may go through a couple of rounds of negotiation, trying to reach an agreement. You may eventually settle on a compromise of $60. Is this a fair price for the seller, who purchased it for $50, and is this a good deal for you, as you only had $20 (in theory) to spend? Is this the best deal for both?

Transferring this to a business context, what we would do is provide transparent justification on *why* a certain amount is fair to us. Without that additional information, fact and legitimacy, it is impossible to break out of the positional bargaining that may actually be a zero-sum game in which value is destroyed, everyone loses and no party wins.

Here are three questions to keep in mind:

- What are the grounds and facts supporting my arguments?
- Am I prepared to probe the legitimacy of the other party's arguments?

- Is my conversation strategy governed by a strong sense of fairness?

Options

Co-creating options is where the fun part starts. You may look at it as a process of choice creation, and cultivating that attitude is a key skill for successful multi-party collaboration.

In negotiations, options refer to any available choices that parties might consider to satisfy their interests, including conditions, contingencies and trades. Because options tend to capitalize on parties' similarities and differences, they can create value in negotiation and improve parties' satisfaction, according to Bruce Patton.[186] Considering and finding options together allows you to broaden the scope of what else is feasible beyond your own and the other party's positions. It acts like a magnifying glass to imagination and shows you opportunities beyond a zero-sum game. By using the principles of legitimacy and interests, you start to see more details and possibilities that were initially hidden behind that one opinion.

In my experience, one of the greatest barriers to effective brainstorming is our tendency to jump to conclusions too quickly. We tend to confuse inventing with decision-making and *option* with *commitment*. This is natural. In a positional bargaining scenario, this is what happens. Like a tennis ball flying back and forth across a court, we shout out quick ideas and options, and close our blinds too quickly on additional options. Here, communication style and choice of words really matter. Practicing open brainstorming, and avoiding closing down a conversation too quickly by asking: "What else can we think of that meets both of our needs?" can be a gratifying strategy.

The advantage of co-creating options together is that it fosters ownership of the idea and increases the chances of sustainable solutions for the future.

There are a couple of strategies to do this practically.

Firstly, when positions seem very far apart, and more barriers than solutions seem to prevail, you can choose to present a few options that allow the other party to add to, criticize or adopt your ideas. This step creates space and represents time well invested, in cases where discussions are getting tense and when stakes are high. As my long-time mentor Charles Barker said in the context of the Camp David Accords, *"It was one of the first steps in getting the parties to understand that success would only come about by crafting a choice to which the other side could say 'yes.'"*[188]

Secondly, if you are lucky and the relationship is in a good and trustworthy place, you may opt to start in a co-creating mode right from the beginning by presenting your own options and asking for additional options simultaneously.

Co-creating options for novel solutions is hard work and takes time! But it can be done, and the outcomes can be outstanding, as some of the high-stake political examples I cited earlier show.

Here are three questions to keep in mind:

- Am I prepared to bring a few early ideas to the table and ask for feedback?

- Can I reflect on and discuss time-contingent solutions that project into the future?
- How can I help the group pause long enough to ensure we find the best possible option?

Alternatives

In the vast majority of cases, working with this playbook leads to a common agreement and a path forward can be sealed.

But, even with a consensus-driven strategy, your primary objective is still to secure your own and your constituents' interests. You will do so with empathy and by listening to all facets of what the other parties have to say. You will ponder the pros and cons of all options on the table. You will make every effort to understand the needs and challenges of the other party or parties to ensure you achieve your shared goal: creating value for all.

Not reaching an agreement would not only risk your own deal, but also your reputation as a collaborative negotiator. In turn, this may negatively impact your relationship with, and any future reliance on, these people.

However, there are times when a mutual agreement is not feasible.

There are a few things you should consider in advance so that you are not caught by surprise. Firstly, carefully prepare your alternatives. What else can be done outside of this group and this set of options, and with whom, to satisfy your interests?

*Being aware of your alternatives conveys
a great deal of confidence.*

Secondly, it may be beneficial to communicate your alternative to the other party or parties, including your BATNA – best alternative to a negotiated agreement, or put differently, best alternative to no agreement.[185] This is where communication and intent become really important. You should only do so with a clear intent in mind, without being perceived as threatening the other party. Despite what you may think, threats have the opposite effect: they erode trust and credibility. The way to do this practically is by describing your choice, showing respect, rephrasing the other party's choice, and emphasizing that your choice is solely to satisfy your interests and not to harm the other party.

Remember the purpose of the long-term relationship for you and your constituents.

Here are three questions to keep in mind:

- What are my alternatives outside of this group and this solution?
- Am I clear on my BATNA and am I prepared to communicate it in a non-threatening way?
- How will I manage the broader communication if this deal isn't working? (patients, policy and so on)

Commitments

This is where agreements risk failing.

"In negotiation, a fundamental challenge is to strike an effective balance between empathy and assertiveness."[193] This is how Robert Mnookin, director at the PON, describes the moment of leaning into your own interests versus giving up certain others in order to safeguard

both your *and* the other party's needs, and the value that a common solution generates. *"Empathy involves effectively understanding your counterpart's perspective and expressing his/her viewpoint in a non-judgmental manner. Assertiveness is the ability to express and advocate for your own needs, interests and perspectives,"* he concludes.

Assertiveness and commitments are integral parts of closing a deal. However, in the joy and relief of reaching an agreement, I have observed many times that parties may forget to commit, look ahead and make plans for actual implementation of the deal.

Particularly when time-bound options are built into the agreement, it is paramount to monitor performance of the deal into the future. Setting clear milestones to progress-check, and holding follow-up meetings to discuss insights around these milestones, is what makes agreements sustainable. This is where true impact and value generation lie. It is the implementation of the deal, not the deal itself, that matters.

*Only once the parties commit will
the solution become a reality.*

It can be hard to keep the momentum going and to manage the impatience of leaders. Delegating some of the operational tasks to project managers and individuals who are responsible for the implementation can be a real game changer. Most of the large-scale public-private partnerships and international coalitions all have a part- or full-time project leader managing these day-to-day aspects. A long-term outlook on logistics, entailing project management and progress checks, will make your agreement a success and one that others want to emulate.

Here are three statements to keep in mind:

- Once we reach an agreement, I will commit.
- I will ask for the other parties' preparedness to commit.
- The agreement will include a project plan to monitor progress and secure long-term success.

RECONNECTING THE DOTS

Multi-party collaborations aren't easy. But when you persist, they work and yield mutual-gain value. Competing priorities, opposing interests, different languages – cooperation means solving all of those differences. Sometimes, we may feel like we're in a never-ending loop with no exit (figure 5.4). Taking the time to probe and unveil what lies behind criticism and objection does take time and patience. But it holds the potential to lead to deep value generation for all.

> *"You can't connect the dots looking forward – you can only connect them looking backwards."*[194]
> ~ STEVE JOBS

Understanding the quandary in health care means realizing that it is not one homogenous sector, like any other industry. If health care were one company, there would be one boss accountable for all the decisions. The five independent constituents in health care, however, more closely resemble a set of *first* violinists trying to get in sync without a conductor. The complexity of five independent,

Figure 5.4. MC Escher's" **Relativity**, illustrating the never-ending loop of partisan perceptions.

disconnected, sometimes opinionated, yet highly talented violinists playing without a conductor requires an effective framework for decision-making. It requires an upgrading of collaborative skills, both on a group level and on an individual leader level.

Multi-party negotiation can work in health care.

Large public-private coalitions, like the COVID-19 example, are demonstrating that the combination of a burning platform, passionate leaders and a strong common objective can break down barriers very effectively. In essence, all the successful partnerships that I have witnessed have three essential components: a strong common purpose, visionary leaders who are able to see the other view, and people who invest in relationships, reconnect the dots and aim to understand each other's problems.

Overcoming complexity in health care is all about connections and forging novel partnerships. It is about breaking down partisan perceptions and replacing them with a mutual-gain co-creation process.

Moving forward, rest assured. This playbook of seven steps is not about giving away all your interests or expertise. On the contrary, by displaying transparency and openness throughout the process, maintaining a patient-centric view, and reminding yourself of the common purpose, both your and the other parties' interests can be met to create value for all. Kessely Hong from the PON advises you to *"create an appealing choice so that honoring your long-term goals meets your short-term interests."*[195]

One of my pivotal learning moments when applying this playbook was a negotiation situation with a national government. It was a negotiation over a new life-saving medicine for a rare blood cancer. There was unanimous agreement on the clinical value of the data and its meaningfulness for patients. Where things started to diverge, and ended up in serious disagreement very quickly, was over the price and the budget impact of this therapy on the health system in this country. I invite you to check out the details in breakout box 4.

BREAKOUT BOX 4: IT IS NEVER A PRICING CONVERSATION

We had spent close to ten years developing this new medicine and finally the results of the controlled clinical trial had demonstrated unprecedented benefit: fifty percent of patients were living six months longer than patients who had been treated with the standard of care.[196] The payer's response was, "*Your data are great, very compelling. But we don't have the money nor the budget to pay for this; here is* our *price proposal.*"

It was four times lower than what we requested. Imagine we had asked for eight dollars — they were ready to pay us two. Our positions were light-years apart and seemed irreconcilable between the key actors. Instantly, there was finger-pointing about who was to blame for this divide. Perceptions of "bad pharma" on the one hand confronted an "avaricious" health authority on the other. We were up against disaster straight away. Not approving this life-saving medicine simply wasn't an option. The obstacles included a limited budget for the payer, and covering drug development investments and ROIs for the company, with the patient standing in the middle.

Eleven months and six negotiation meetings later, we eventually found a way to approve this medicine at an ROI that was viable for the company and, from a future budget impact perspective, was acceptable to the payer. What happened and what was the secret sauce to success?

As outlined earlier, the starting point was to anchor our conversation around a common *purpose*, which was granting access to this new life-saving medicine. Secondly, it was only by eliciting *interests* behind the initial price rejection that we would unveil a whole different layer of issues in our *relationship*. This was not done in one conversation or one meeting. This required strong communication skills, empathy, listening, and not using threatening behavior or feeling threatened (which could have happened easily multiple times in various encounters). Great effort was made over many weeks and months. Good things take time. What we were working through, meeting after meeting, were layers of institutional mistrust that had accumulated over time between the governmental agency and the pharmaceutical company. *"You can't trust these guys,"* is what both parties typically said behind closed doors. However, once we started to gain some common ground between the individual people at the table, nurturing some early, fragile signs of trust, we realized that there was no controversy at all regarding the value of the product. What we discovered, instead, were issues around budget concerns, reliable forecasts, and honoring past and present commitments. We did not have a pricing issue. We had a serious trust issue in our relationship, with real and perceived broken commitments stemming from previous interactions.

None of the people at the negotiation table had been present during past interactions. But the distrust was there.

This story shows the importance of taking time, eliciting interests with legitimacy and creating options within the relationship, while always remaining focused on the common purpose.

Reading this chapter, you may think, "Nice story. Nice theory. But this won't work in my case. You have no idea how difficult the people are that *I am* dealing with!"

Indeed, each situation and circumstance is different. Dealing with difficult people, or simply finding the time, patience and willingness of others to engage in a novel path, is hard work. However, this proven playbook holds real power to catalyze mindsets, cultures and outcomes. Ultimately, it is more of a technique, a mindset and a philosophy than a rigid, formal process. It works even if only one of the parties applies it, and it presents itself as a perfect playbook to nurture bottom-up initiatives.

Conversely, you may think, "Well, that sounds all very simple, almost trivial. I can do that; I listen all the time. Big deal!" As with many new skills in life, and behaviors we plan to adopt, the devil of collaborative negotiation lies in the detail – and operational implementation. Some of the most experienced negotiators have rarely seen a negotiation anchored in a strong purpose fail because parties technically weren't able to agree. The majority of negotiations fail not because there aren't good options in terms of solutions, but because parties fail to prepare.

Curiosity, empathy and preparation are the keys to success, and the best predictors for positive outcomes in multi-party collaborations.

TOP TAKEAWAYS FROM CHAPTER FIVE

☑   We don't have an issue of innovative solutions in health care. Rather, it's important to understand how positions, opinions and partisan perceptions pose frequent hurdles in the health care ecosystem, including unnecessary conflict.

☑   Overcoming bottlenecks means leaving comfort zones, and requires a fundamental mindset shift. If leaders can adopt a deep collaborative skillset, such as the interest-based playbook of seven steps, they can mediate conversations with empathy, reconnect the dots and forge novel partnerships.

☑   This technique has been proven successful in the realm of political disputes, business conflicts and interpersonal relationships. There is no reason why it can't be used to develop novel multi-party solutions in health care.

Bringing it all together in a collaborative, value-based and smart *Tango for Five*

"The world is not going to change unless
we are willing to change ourselves."

~ RIGOBERTA MENCHÚ TUM (1992 NOBEL PEACE PRIZE WINNER)

PUSHING THE RESET BUTTON IN HEALTH CARE

In the wake of COVID-19, health care will never be the same. The flaws and gaps that existed before the pandemic rose to the surface and became visible to everyone. Yet, I am thinking that in ten years' time, many of the current problems will feel like distant memories of the past.

But we won't solve these problems without considerable effort. There is no magic bullet that will send us in the right direction. We have to hit that "Reset" button ourselves, as leaders in health care.

"You can't expect a different outcome by applying the same experiment," as researchers say. We have to radically change the way we work in this industry and embrace the disruptions that COVID-19 has brought about. We have to seize the moment, radically change the way we operate in health care, and perpetuate those changes long term. Rebuilding a sustainable, resilient and patient-centered system of health is what we have to deliver for our future and the next generation. However, the only way to reset health care is by doing it together. That is, by abandoning the solo dance and learning and dancing a *Tango for Five*.

Before moving on to summarize my top ten focus areas of action, let me start by saying that *change starts with realizing what the problem is.*

You can't fix the car if you don't know what is broken. You can't heal an illness if you haven't done a proper diagnosis. Same with system errors. Many misunderstandings and misperceptions circulate around what the root causes are for our broken health care systems. Looking at the daily headlines, what I am not seeing is a balanced view. If blaming one single actor would lead us to the solution that fixes health care, why hasn't it worked so far? Reporting on skyrocketing drug prices, condemning "bad" pharma for reaping financial benefits, blaming payers for keeping budgets tight, and criticizing physicians and hospitals for reaping benefits on procedures, is all missing the point.

We are facing a twofold quandary in health care: an imbalance between innovation and affordability, and an all-time-high level of mistrust and dysconnectivity between the top five actors: patients, providers, pharma, payers and policymakers. Remember figure 1.2 in the first chapter, illustrating the imbalance? In order to restore this balance, as shown in figure vi below, we need to fundamentally change the way we work in health care. We can do this by swapping transactionally focused, short-term FFS structures with strategic and collaborative solutions co-created by the top five actors. No one can act in isolation. Yet, the reality is that a group of solo dancers *are* making decisions in isolation. None of this is intentional. It has not been for a lack of trying to modernize the system, and get a grasp on this upward spiral of cost and downward spiral of quality in care. In my thirty-year career in this industry, everyone whom I have encountered – be it in the public health sector or in the private life sciences sector – has chosen to work here for a reason.

Let's harness that power.

> *"... a nation that isn't broken, but simply unfinished."*

This is what young poet Amanda Gorman wrote in the poem she recited at the inauguration ceremony for the 46th president of the United States.[198] It is how I wish to look at our health care transformation. Despite all the big problems, there is also much good will among its main actors, and so much positive energy in the system, that I have started thinking of it as "simply unfinished".

Figure vi: Restoring the quandary of health care.

Note that the pebbles in this picture don't necessarily depict one actor or one aspect, but rather illustrate the complexities of various factors that need to align in health care in order to achieve optimal innovation and outcomes with optimal affordability and efficiencies.

What we need is everyone taking action and thinking BIG.

This is what this book is all about: broadening perspectives on what the problems are, and what the solutions can be. Cooperation on all levels, and focusing on value for all instead of benefits for some, will be the new competitive advantage. It occurs in a crosstalk between local leaders and local projects in the public and private sectors, and is endorsed by governments and lawmakers. Switching our culture from analog, hierarchical and transactional to smart, digital and strategic represents the new dawn in health care.

Figure vii. Bringing solutions to health care means going BIG.

TOP TEN FOCUS AREAS FOR
CHANGE IN HEALTH CARE

Let me leave you with my top ten key takeaways for a better health care system of the future. Remember, as leaders, we are being judged for our actions and not our words.

Figure viii. Top ten focus areas for change in health care.

FROM COMPETITION TO COOPERATION IN HEALTH CARE
Top Ten Focus Areas to Effectively Dance a _Tango for Five_

1.	**Patient Centricity.**	Outcomes and VBHC.
2.	**Health Literacy.**	Patient Empowerment and Education.
3.	**Care Coordination.**	Primary Care and Future of Hospitals.
4.	**Incentives Reform.**	Taking off the Pressure to Produce Revenues.
5.	**Prevention.**	Health Continuum and SODH.
6.	**Digital Transformation.**	Deep Medicine and Smart Hospitals.
7.	**Digital Literacy.**	AI, DTx and m-health.
8.	**Leadership.**	Mindset and Culture.
9.	**Negotiation Skills.**	Playbook to Orchestrate a _Tango for Five_.
10.	**Disruptors.**	Agility and Innovation in light of Megatrends.

Note: In the supplementary materials at the back of this book, you'll find a list of guiding questions related to this list.

1. Patient centricity

Value starts with the patient. Let's remember that we _all_ are patients, sooner or later, in one way or another. As such, health care is a core pillar in our societies. From early VBHC projects, we are noticing a massive shift toward a more empathetic and collaborative system of health. _"Start with the goal of the patient, don't set it for them, but align with their interests,"_ is what Hanna, as a type 1 diabetes patient, calls out to her providers.[199,200] Putting the patient at the center is the True North, as a dialogue around patient-focused outcomes naturally galvanizes teamwork. And what you also can appreciate, as shown by all the examples cited in this book, is that this model works to re-gain efficiencies and produce economic gains, too.

Value means breakthrough solutions. Patients, payers and providers need to see substantial clinical and societal meaningfulness in order to adopt and pay for innovation. In the future, new medicines and solutions need to demonstrate transformational potential instead of incremental steps. One disruptive idea, which emerged during one of my podcast conversations on academia-pharma collaborations, was to start any new drug development project with a strategic, patient-centric advisory board before embarking on the lengthy journey of drug development.[201]

People pay for what they value. Therefore, copycat and refurbished products under a new brand name won't be good enough anymore. Just delivering products, without enhancing outcomes, won't suffice. Conversely, pharma, payers, policymakers and civic society need to work together to decide what they value most. New payment models and reimbursement reforms will need to answer the question: how much do we value the treatment of chronic illness and the cure of life-threatening diseases?

2. Health literacy

Empowered patients are a source of untapped potential. If we want to help people better understand their health conditions, and empower them to manage their own health, we need to upgrade investments into education. As Hanna explained in reference to her own journey, it was only once she understood the impact of diabetes on her body, and that there were ways for her to avoid disastrous experiences and frequent visits to the ER, that she fully embraced the responsibility of managing her condition. Investment in patients' understanding of their diagnosis, treatments and personal choices (lifestyle changes) is what we generally refer to as improving health literacy.

We have seen in chapter three how scholars and practitioners around the world have long agreed that the fundamental switch from a fee-for-service system to a model that rewards outcomes is the way to go. As such, VBHC is the compass that is built around just that purpose – helping the patient, including helping them maintain their best possible level of health. It incentivizes the patient as much as doctors to co-create solutions that work for them, achieving better outcomes overall.

With the advent of digitalization in health care, wearables, apps and smart devices finally make patient empowerment a reality. Measuring one's own symptoms and sharing alerts with providers is what helps patients embrace new possibilities. Although no one wants to be regularly reminded that they are sick, new creative solutions, like self-reward systems within health apps, are emerging to overcome that hurdle. M-health forces us to think differently about the whole value chain, and appreciate the fact that patients are moving into the driver's seat of their own health, choosing the solutions at their fingertips that provide value to them.

3. Care coordination

Optimizing care coordination generates value. Today, care is fragmented and uncoordinated in many places. We all experience the hassle of navigating doctors' appointments, hospital corridors and repetitive tests. There is a high likelihood that you yourself, or someone in your life, has lived through such an experience, maybe even recently. Not only is the lack of coordination a nuisance to the patient journey, but it is foremost time-consuming and costly.

What all the VBHC real-world examples are showing is that the focus on patient outcomes automatically drives better care coordination between the main actors. Doctors, nurses, pharmacists, social workers, physiotherapists, and whoever else is needed to drive clinical and societal impact.

As care becomes increasingly patient-centric and home-based, the role of general practitioners and smart hospitals needs to evolve. Once longer-term, more holistic care is on equal footing as procedures, the time spent supporting patients in navigating their own illnesses will be attractive to GPs again. Many countries are showing that this model actually works. The evolution of hospitals into digitally powered institutions, focused on highly specialized and episodic care that is not available in community settings, is a likely scenario. As part of this trend, they may expand their role in effectively and swiftly supporting matters of public health interest, such as the COVID-19 crisis.

For example, today it is impossible to assess the dollars spent and the health benefit gained along a patient journey from start to finish. It is impossible to measure the total cost for one cycle of care. It is impossible to follow one dollar of product sold by a pharmaceutical manufacturer to the end user because of innumerable intermediaries all benefiting from that dollar, but not adding any new value per se. What we need are solutions that fix the principles behind it (VBHC) and the infrastructure to support it (digital). In order to support the transition from volume to value, we need to put the same value tag on care that we used to put on procedures, products and services.

4. Incentives reform

We need a seismic shift in our incentives structure. In order to push VBHC from theory to practice, with patient empowerment and care coordination at its center, we need a fundamental reform of our reward structures. If you are incentivized on cost, number of procedures and length of visit, what you will produce is more cost, more procedures and more visits. We need to alleviate the pressure to produce. It leads to burnout and frustration, decreases quality, and distorts the conversation on progress. You can't make progress in a zero-sum game.

However, if you switch the rules of the game, incentivizing on how well patients feel, what the end result of a procedure is, and how well a treatment is working, this will automatically change the dialogue. As we have seen, *value* instead of *volume* in health care is not mere theory, but actually works in real-life settings. The way the team at Intermountain Healthcare in the US has been successful over the past twenty years provides an example. They split the overall organization's profitability into one part that deals with acute care and short-term-driven patient flows, and a second part that is focused on long-term care to generate better health for the overall population of patients.[202]

This takes time. And it cannot be accomplished by one actor alone.

Given the complexity and interconnectivity of the health care eco-system, this will only become a reality if policymakers, providers, payers and patients work together and align to implement a novel incentive structure. In the past, we lacked the tools to measure a total cost for one cycle of care and to process these massive amounts of data. Now, with the advent of VBHC frameworks and the digital revolution, we have all we need. The missing link is the individual will and the critical mass of leaders deciding to implement these tools.

5. Prevention

Maintaining good health is less expensive than treating illness. Solving the quandary in health care requires rebalancing the fixing and preventing. Patient empowerment, digitalization and VBHC incentives all move the needle toward a renewed focus on protecting health and preventing illness in the first place. Naturally, in the FFS system of the past, more was better. There was no room to reward "doing nothing or less". It has become ingrained into our culture of "a pill for everything".

However, one key factor that can address the imbalance of innovation and affordability is lifestyle changes. It has been long recognized that social determinants of health have eight times more impact on people's health than any pill or procedure could ever have. Therefore, the role of policymakers, governments and medical professionals is to equally invest in emotional, societal, educational and work-related measures in order to redress the resilience of our health care systems.

Several countries are leading the way, with 2030 health agendas setting forth strong, balanced strategies that aim to move the needle along the whole health continuum – from prevention to acute and chronic care, survivorship and terminal care. Particularly in light of the three megatrends of the future – aging, chronic diseases and mental health – investments on the earliest part of the spectrum are a smart choice.[203,204]

6. Digital transformation

Finally, the Fourth Industrial Revolution is catching up with health care. It gained momentum at the start of the new millennium, but was really ignited through the massive disruption of COVID-19. Seemingly overnight, it forced doctors, hospitals and drug developers into using telehealth. Truth be told, remote patient consults and monitoring were possible long ago, but they had not really been adopted broadly, either by providers or patients, because of lacking incentives and culture. There was no checkbox in the prior billing systems, nor did doctors or patients really believe they would derive full benefit of the visit when delivered through a videoscreen.

"As machines get smarter and take on suitable tasks, humans might actually find it easier to be more human," says Dr Eric Topol in his landmark book on the topic, *Deep Medicine*.[105]

From a system's perspective, the way we will integrate the human touch into deep medicine will evolve. The reality is likely to be somewhere in the middle: condensing distance and time through telehealth, and complementing the care for emotional needs via face-to-face encounters. Ultimately, digitalization is here to make health care, our health systems and operational ways of working more efficient. The demand is high and the solutions are here to streamline processes, supply chains and communication channels between doctors, hospitals, pharmacies, payers and drug developers. From a systems perspective, the upgrading of IT infrastructure, the wide-area implementation of EHR, and the automation of repetitive tasks all promise to make health care cheaper, faster and more human.

7. Digital literacy

Learning how to use digital tools comes easily to the younger generations, but it may be a challenge for baby boomers and members of generations X and Y. Many of my own colleagues still prefer using their handwritten notes instead of typing on a computer, let alone juggling keyboards on tiny mobile devices and wearables. You may think this is not a major issue, but the statistics suggest otherwise. For example, despite great efforts by the German government and great general enthusiasm about modernization, ninety-three percent of health care providers in Germany still use paper charts, suggesting there needs to be a massive movement to enhance digital literacy.[179]

In light of the aging population, the use of m-health and telehealth needs to take into account the special needs of the elderly, including their reduced cognitive function. How many elderly people are confident using smartphones and DTx apps, and attending video appointments? As such, the role of the caregiver as an additional end user comes into focus. The overall success of adoption will depend on their involvement, both in the development and deployment stages.

In addition to creating a broad basic skill for end users of m-health, we will see the creation of totally new jobs and subspecialties in the realms of digital health, AI and ML, both in the private and public sectors. In the future, software developers will be working hand-in-glove with clinicians, payers and drug developers. AI-powered federated learning will transform the way we innovate in medicine. AI will make innovations much more efficient. It is the enabler to bring personalized medicine to our doorsteps, via precision diagnostics, prevention and treatment.

As in other sectors where digital is revolutionizing the way we work, the fear of AI replacing humans is real. As a result, investing in human upskilling and reskilling is part of most long-term plans. The benefits are obvious. In its "Future of Jobs Report 2020," the WEF estimates that eighty-five million jobs will be displaced while ninety-seven million new jobs will be created across twenty-six countries by 2025, driving an overall productivity increase of twenty-six percent.[205,206] In health care, the efficiency gains cannot be underestimated. Shaving off the billions of dollars and decades of time spent on traditional drug development will help to restore the balance between innovation and affordability.

8. Leadership

Leaders make change happen. Leadership is not about executives and managers only. It touches everyone. It can be learned and is a matter of taking responsibility. What I find particularly encouraging, when looking at the plethora of VBHC projects, is the fact that change in health care can start with small projects. It is as much a top-down framework as a bottom-up one.

From an organizational standpoint, companies, organizations and teams are made up of people. It's no different in health care. As much as we need fundamental systems and policy changes, these changes won't happen if leaders don't drive them. It requires both a personal mindset change and a collective culture change. Moving from competing to cooperation requires a whole new set of leadership skills. The general trend in a digitalized, value-driven and collaborative workplace is toward de-emphasizing hierarchical, top-down and technical skills in favor of collaborative, integrative and complex problem-solving skills. "The Future of Jobs Report 2020" states, *"In particular, self-management skills such as mindfulness, meditation, gratitude and kindness are among the top ten focus areas of those in employment in contrast to the more technical skills which were in-focus in 2019."*[205]

There is huge opportunity for the private sector to cross-fertilize with the public sector when it comes to leadership. As part of its

"Closing the Skills Gap" project, launched in the wake of COVID-19, the WEF states, *"forty-two percent of the skills demand for jobs across all industries will change between 2018 and 2022. The private sector is a leading stakeholder in managing this transformation through collective action on future-oriented skills development, thereby serving as a critical partner to governments and education and training providers to enable opportunities for all and to meet the needs of labor markets."* [207]

9. Negotiation skills

Leaders who sing from the same song sheet make change happen together. Society's expectations of health care have dramatically changed as a result of the pandemic. It is imperative for health care leaders to embrace change and reform our health care systems to achieve more equitable value for all. However, overcoming these legal, regulatory and risk-averse operational barriers to collaboration lies with each individual actor. In the quandary of health care, there is no one single conductor. It takes five to tango and it takes all to agree on a common purpose in order to implement all the required institutional, systems and infrastructure changes. Hence, equipping leaders with a skillset that allows them to bridge their divides – and help them reconcile varying interests, needs and objectives – is what will make theory a reality in the everyday lives of doctors, payers, policymakers, pharma leaders and patients.

The good news is that many of the necessary ingredients are already on hand, as outlined throughout this book. But ultimately, it is the *people* who need to adopt a skillset anchored in empathy and self-awareness. As demonstrated by the interest-based playbook of seven principles, taking into account the other view opens the doors to cooperation.

To bring back the concepts of Pablo Pugliese, the smart tango dancer, coach and leadership expert, by adopting a common vocabulary, such as interests, legitimacy and alternatives, we can forge new relationships, communicate novel options, and commit to sustainable solutions. Together.

In a landmark business article titled "The Rules of Co-opetition", published by *Harvard Business Review*, the authors state, "*There are many reasons for competitors to cooperate. At the simplest level, it can be a way to save costs and avoid duplication of effort. ... Cooperation is an overall win-win, but splitting the gains is a zero-sum game.*"[208] It is through cooperation that we build trust. Once we trust each other, we can dissolve frustrations and get back to work to make change happen.

10. Disruptors

Adapt and prepare for disruptors, as health care will never be as it was before. This does not only include the shift to value-based incentives and digitalized solutions. It also means disruption of the way we have looked at this industry in the first place. This is what Michael Porter refers to as the "threat of substitutes", or new market entrants, in his landmark paper, "The Five Competitive Forces That Shape Strategy."[209]

New entrants look and feel very different. They don't resemble typical health actors: hospitals, pharma companies, pharmacists or health insurers. They come by the name of Amazon Pharmacy, Apple Research App, Google Health Studies and Microsoft Cloud for Healthcare, to name only a few.[109] Widely built on interoperable software platforms, they bring agility to supply chains, distribution, clinical research, telehealth and m-health solutions. Focusing on the consumer need, they tailor providers, pharma and patients in a direct-to-consumer fashion, and virtually break down traditional and sequential value chain and drug development cycles. We are on the verge of the Fifth Industrial Revolution, which will connect our minds with our AI/ML-powered machines, as we are already seeing with the likes of Elon Musk's latest project, Neuralink, a technology that can record and stimulate signals from thousands of sites in the brain.[210]

For now, in health care, the pace of change continues to exponentially disrupt traditional ways of developing and delivering care. Since health is a precious diamond, we need to be careful here. There are inherent risks with non-health care professionals driving solutions such as "Dr Google" and non-health expert social media influencers. Errors and inconsistencies need to be managed between the existing workforce and new entrants. Harnessing these developments in a collaborative manner will bring enhanced value to all actors in the ecosystem. In contrast, working in a competitive manner and bargaining on resources is likely to fall short when it comes to these agile, fast and disruptive entrants. What we need is for new entrants and existing health care professionals to work hand-in-glove, proactively involving policymakers and civic society to further elevate patient-centric and value-based systems of health for the twenty-first century.

WHAT EVERYONE CAN DO TO DANCE AN INTEGRATED *TANGO FOR FIVE*

Let's be realistic. The forces resisting change are enormous. The powers at play are gigantic. The variety of actors is so heterogeneous:

doctors, patients, pharma, insurers and government. The problem is big. Many of us feel overwhelmed and helpless in light of the task at hand. With this in mind, our only option is to work together. There is no better moment than now, as we begin to emerge from a pandemic, to tackle the problem once and for all.

———

We all share responsibility. Now it is up to health care leaders – us, you, me – to make change happen. Together in a Tango for Five. Let's dance!

———

ACKNOWLEDGMENTS

*"Writing is easy. All you have to do is
cross out the wrong words."*

~ MARC TWAIN

Writing a book is quite a journey. For me, it was a journey into myself, a journey back in time, and a journey back to many memories with beloved people and enriching encounters along the way. Many mentors, colleagues and friends have forged my experiences, both in the clinics and in business, many of which I shared in this book. "It takes a village to raise a child," as the African proverb goes. It certainly takes a village to drive changes in health care – and it certainly takes a village to write a book about it. No one can do it alone. Therefore, I am incredibly grateful to so many who have accompanied me over these wonderful past three decades at the forefront of health care, and over the past year researching and working on this book.

Let me start at the end, as you and I are holding this *Tango for Five* in our hands.

Firstly, this book never would have come to fruition without my fabulous editor, Kelly Irving. She is the mastermind behind transforming a great idea into a tangible piece of paper, just like a magician who pulls a rabbit out of her hat. Working with Kelly allowed me to gain clarity about what it was I wanted to say, share and bring forward from my own experiences. For anyone who always wanted to write *that one book*, I highly recommend seeking her advice on how to actually get it done. Her author academy is a sounding board and wonderful community that helped me understand I wasn't alone with my feelings of uncertainty and that empty, white page staring at me.

Secondly, I am very appreciative of the team at Grammar Factory Publishing: Scott MacMillan, Michelle Stevenson, Jake Creasey, Carolyn Jackson, Julia Kuris and Dania Zafar all of whom have been outstanding in providing fruitful and agile support to a first-time author like myself. Casting a word document into a final book setup from front to back takes a village and is a true art!

Thirdly, my gratitude goes to the many friends and colleagues who have given me the gift of their time to review many rounds of early- and late-stage manuscript drafts. Special thanks goes to Sarah Richards, who has been incredibly patient with me, particularly when I took my first steps as a writer sharing this *Tango for Five*, initially drawn up as a concept on paper. Her advice on how to tell a compelling story, and not just (scientific) facts, was quite a revelation to me, and as I developed a new skill I also developed a new passion for writing. Additionally, my sincere thank you for insightful feedback, text and graphic support goes to: Adrien Kaiser, Andrea Frey, Blaine Rada, Céline Faivre-Delaloye, Charles Barker, Gilles Lunzenfichter, Géraldine van Kaenel, Guy Downes, Hanna Boëthius, Katrin Rupalla, Ilka Dekan, Lea Dias, Nakisa Serry, Nadav Zadok, Olivia Zollinger, Pascal Deschaseaux, Pascal Kurz, Philippe van Holle, Suzanne Robinson and Thomas Clozel.

Overall, it also takes a village to build a successful career. I have been fortunate enough to have many mentors, colleagues and advising friends who have shaped who I am as a doctor today.

My gratitude goes to the patients in my clinic who have taught me humility, patience and resilience. It is the most fulfilling experience to see a patient and their family leave my office with a smile, hope and signs of relief, when maybe one hour earlier they had entered that same office full of fear, anxiety and devastation after a terrible diagnosis. Helping patients face their illness, by working together to co-create the best possible path for them to reach optimal quality *and* quantity of life, has remained the guiding compass throughout my career.

There are far too many dear mentors and colleagues to name them all individually here. However, there are five leaders who have been instrumental at gatekeeping moments of my career. Without their precious advice and endorsement, I would not have been able to grow outside my comfort zone, and discover new aspects in my profession and in my life. Firstly, my gratitude goes to Dr Benjamin Winograd, who had the vision to lift me over from academia to pharmaceuticals and see the potential that this would open up to me. Without him, the *Tango for Five* would not have become visible to me (beyond the provider and patient perspectives). Second, it took the mastermind of Philippe van Holle to propel me from Europe to Asia, and help me to make a dream come true. My two years in Korea have been life-changing, on a personal as well as a professional level. Thirdly, Axel Glasmacher was another key person who supported my journey several times, not only with my move to Korea, but also between R&D and Medical Affairs functions along my industry career.

Fourthly, it was thanks to Dr Jean-Pierre Bizzarri that I have been able to fully embrace the power of academia-industry relationships. Without his visionary leadership, we would not have been able to deliver new advances in the realm of cancer drug development in record time. He taught me how to truly dance a *Tango for Five* and create a trustworthy atmosphere in which an equitable partnership can unfold between academia and industry. Lastly, I owe much of my business expertise to Marie-France Tschudin. She was instrumental in steering me toward a full-circle experience in the industry, putting her trust in me as a commercial leader of one of the main franchises in the European and Middle Eastern regions. This has been one of the most enriching, enjoyable experiences of my career. Without her far-sightedness and empowerment, I would not have been able to expand my medical expertise into the realms of payer, business and policy perspectives, which are so instrumental in bringing life-saving treatments to the patient's bedside.

As I am writing these last lines of *It Takes Five to Tango*, my thoughts go to my parents, Lydia and Oswald Völter. They have been my earliest supporters on my path to become a doctor since my childhood days in the Black Forest. It was my father's sister, Renate Völter, who brought me to that first hospital doorstep. And it was my father's mother, my late grandmother Senta Völter, who, as one of the first women entering medical school in 1918, became a female physician role model to me. It was she who taught me how to do medical stiches on a lunch table napkin, using her surgical toolkit from the original doctor's purse she carried as a GP during the Second World War. Without my parents, I would not have found the courage, resilience and energy to pursue this long and sometimes rocky path to becoming a health care professional. In addition to their infinite love, I also owe them my passion for discovering and traveling the world. Since my early childhood, they have opened me up to new languages, cultures and countries.

Last but not least, this book is dedicated to Dr Roger Stupp, my fabulous tango partner in life. He is the love of my life and I owe him everything since I entered my residency in cancer care. Not only was he my first attending supervisor in oncology, he is also an incredibly good mentor in clinical research and clinical care. Always focused on doing the right thing, the sharpness of his thinking – and his fundamental sense of equality – continues to serve as a North Star for me. I feel fortunate to share my life, my passion for patients, and my dedication to science with him. I am forever thankful for his support, encouragement and love.

GLOSSARY

Glossary of abbreviations

ADHD: Attention-deficit/hyperactivity disorder

AI: Artificial intelligence

AMR: Antimicrobial resistance

ASCT: Autologous stem cell transplant

ACTIV: Accelerating COVID-19 Therapeutic Interventions and Vaccines

B2B: Business to business

B2C: Business to consumer

CART: Chimeric antigen receptor T-cell

CMS: Center for Medicaid & Medicare Services (US)

D-Health: Digital Health

DRG: Diagnosis-related group

DTx: Digital therapeutic

ECB: European Central Bank

EHR: Electronic health record

EMR: Electronic medical record

EPR: Electronic patient record

EMA: European Medicines Agency

ER: Emergency room

FDA: Food and Drug Administration (US)

FedAI: Federated AI based learning

FFS: Fee-for-service (system)

GDP: Gross domestic product

GP: General practitioner

HHS: Health and Human Services (US)

HNP: Harvard Negotiation Project

ICHOM: International Consortium for Health Outcomes Measurement

IFM: Intergroupe Francophone du Myélome

IMF: International Monetary Fund

IMiDs®: Proprietary small molecule, orally available, that modulates the immune system

IPU: Integrated patient unit

M-Health: Mobile Health

ML: Machine learning

MM: Multiple myeloma

NHS: National Health Service (UK)

NIH: National Institute of Health (US)

OECD: Organisation for Economic Co-operation and Development

OSH: Oak Street Health

PON: Program on Negotiation

PPP: Public-private partnership

PROMS: Patient reported outcomes measures

RA: Rheumatoid arthritis

R&D: Research and development

ROI: Return-on-investment

RPM: Remote patient monitoring

RVU: Relative value unit

SDOH: Social determinants of health

TDABC: Time-driven-activity-based-costing

VBHC: Value-based health care

VC: Venture capital

WEF: World Economic Forum

WHO: World Health Organization

WMA: World Medical Association

REFERENCES

FOREWORD

1. The King's Fund. The Department of Health and Social Care's budget. December 2020: https://www.kingsfund.org.uk.

PREFACE

2. Ezekiel J. Emanuel. Which Country Has the World's Best Health Care? (2020) Public Affairs New York.
3. Zeev E. Neuwirth. Reframing Healthcare: A Roadmap for Creating Disruptive Change (2019) Advantage Media Group.

INTRODUCTION – Prioritizing health care for the benefit of our economies and societies

4. Lauren Bauer et al. Ten Facts about COVID-19 and the U.S. Economy. (2020) www.hamiltonprject.org.
5. Sage J. Kim et al. Social Vulnerability and Racial Inequality in COVID-19 Deaths in Chicago. Health Education & Behavior (2020); Vol 47(4): 509–513.
6. www.pabloynoel.com.

CHAPTER 1 – Restoring the broken balance between innovation and affordability

7. Jill Sederstrom. Does Value Mean Doing Less? ASH Clinical News (2020) Jan, p. 12.
8. @GretaThunberg on Twitter (2020), 27 Nov.
9. Natasa Mihailovic et al. Review of Diagnosis-Related Group-Based Financing of Hospital Care. Health Serv Res Manag Epidemiol. (2016) published online 12 May.

10. Health at a Glance 2019: OECD Indicators. (2019) OECD Publishing, Paris.

11. U.S. Health Care Puts $4 Trillion in All the Wrong Places. Bloomberg Health Law & Business News. (2020) 11 Jun.

12. Matej Mikulic. (2020), 25 May in www.statista.com.

13. Matej Mikulic. (2020), 10 Feb in www.statista.com.

14. Siegel R.L. et al. CA Cancer J Clin (2021); 71(1):7-33.

15. www.seer.gov/statfacts/html/mulmy.html.

16. www.seer.gov/statfacts/html/breast.html.

17. Shaji K. Kumar et al. Continued improvement in survival in multiple myeloma: changes in early mortality and outcomes in older patients. Leukemia (2014); 28: 1122-1128.

18. Arthur Bobin et al. Multiple Myeloma: An Overview of the Current and Novel Therapeutic Approaches in 2020. Cancers (2020); 12:2885.

19. www.revlimidhcp.com.

20. www.celgene.com.

21. www.myelome.fr.

22. David Cameron et al. 11 years' follow-up of trastuzumab after adjuvant chemotherapy in HER2-positive early breast cancer: final analysis of the HERceptin Adjuvant (HERA) trial. Lancet (2017); 389(10075):1195-1205.

23. Kathryn C. Arbour et al. Systemic Therapy for Locally Advanced and Metastatic Non-Small Cell Lung Cancer: A Review. JAMA (2019); 322(8):764-774.

24. Margaret K. Callahan et al. Nivolumab Plus Ipilimumab in Patients With Advanced Melanoma: Updated Survival, Response and Safety Data in a Phase I Dose-Escalation Study. J Clin Oncol (2018); 36(4):391-398.

25. Bertrand Coiffier et al. Long-term outcome of patients in the LNH-98.5 trial, the first randomized study comparing

rituximab-CHOP to standard CHOP chemotherapy in DLBCL patients: a study by the Groupe d'Etudes des Lymphomes de l'Adulte. N Engl J Med (2010); 116(12):2040-5.

26. Andrew Briggs. Effective Use of Health Technology – Assessment to Maximize Market Access: Start Early and Update Often. Pharma Voice (2011) p. 60.

27. Olivier Wouters et al. Estimated Research and Development Investment Needed to Bring a New Medicine to Market, 2009-2018. JAMA (2020); 323(9):844-853.

28. A Decade Marked By Outrage Over Drug Prices. www.npr.org (2019) 31 Dec.

29. Gerry Greenstone. The revival of thalidomide: From tragedy to therapy. BC Medical journal (2011); 53(5):230-233.

30. www.contergan.grunenthal.info/thalidomid.

31. Judah Folkman. Tumor angiogenesis: Therapeutic implications. N Engl J Med (1971); 285:1182-1186.

32. Seema Singhal et al. Antitumor activity of thalidomide in refractory multiple myeloma. N Engl J Med (1999); 341:1565-1571.

33. Philippe Moreau et al. Current trends in autologous stem-cell transplantation for myeloma in the era of novel therapies. J Clin Oncol (2011); 29:1898-1906.

34. Mark Pearson. Tackling Wasteful Spending on Health. Learning from OECD countries' experience. Presentation at the King's Fund in London (2017) 10 Jan, available at oecd.org.

35. Stefan Kapferer, Deputy Secretary General. Value-based health care in Europe. Collaborating for a healthy future. Available at www.oecd.org/health.

36. Marty Makary. The Price We Pay: What Broke American Health Care – and How to Fix It. (2019) Bloomsbury.

37. Trends in healthcare spending. www.ama-assn.org.

38. Apoorva Rama. Policy Research Perspectives. National Health Expenditures, 2018: Spending Growth Remains Steady Even With Increases in Private Health Insurance and Medicare Spending. (2020) American Medical Association.

39. Distribution of National Health Expenditures, by Type of Service (in Billions), 2012 and 2023. Kaiser Family Foundation (2014) 23 Oct, available at kff.org.

40. https://www.swissinfo.ch/eng/health-and-finance_healthcare-expenses-keep-rising-in-switzerland/45746782.

41. https://www.srf.ch/news/schweiz/kostensenkung-bundesrat-schlaegt-umstrittene-massnahmen-im-gesundheitswesen-vor?wt_mc_o=srf.share.app.srf-app.unknown.

42. Thomas Koulopoulos. Reimaging Healthcare. How the smartsourcing revolution will drive the future of healthcare and refocus it on what matters most, the patient. (2020) Post Hill Press.

CHAPTER 2 – Strengthening the interconnectivity of the top five actors in health care

43. James J. Lipsky. Antiretroviral drugs for AIDS. Lancet (1996); 348(9030):800-3.

44. Hervé Zylberberg. Tritherapy for Human Immunodeficiency Virus Infection Does Not Modify Replication of Hepatitis C Virus in Coinfected Subjects. Clinical Infectious Diseases (1998); 26(5):1104–1106.

45. Raymond B. Weiss et al. An On-Site Audit of the South African Trial of High-Dose Chemotherapy for Metastatic Breast Cancer and Associated Publications. J Clin Oncol (2001); 19(11):2771-7.

46. Scott Gottlieb. Breast cancer researcher accused of serious scientific misconduct. West J Med. 2000 Apr; 172(4): 229.

47. Kristina Gaddy. The Fraudulent Study That Killed Thousands of

Breast Cancer Patients. (2016) 4 Dec, available at ozy.com.

48. Renata Brentjes. Patient as an innovative partner. (2020) 16 Nov, available at www.youtube.com.

49. Robert Pearl. The Unspoken Causes of Physician Burnout. (2019) 8 Jul, available at forbes.com.

50. Medscape National Physician Burnout & Suicide Report 2020: The Generational Divide. (2020) 15 Jan, available at www. medscape.com.

51. Pamela Hartzband. Physician Burnout, Interrupted. N Engl J Med (2020); 382:2485-2487.

52. Eric D. Tetzlaff. Burnout on the rise among oncology physician assistants. (2020) 15 Jul, available at www.helio.com.

53. Arthur Olesch. Digital Health in 2020. About Digital Health (2020), available at www.aboutdigitalhealth.com.

54. Bill Siwicki. Pandemic-era burnout: Nurses in the trenches say technology hurts and helps. Healthcare IT News (2020) 9 Nov, available at www.healthcareitnews.com.

55. Understanding RVUs, available at https://bhmpc.com.

56. RVU's Killer Burden on Physicians. Journal of Medicine. (2014) 1 May.

57. The Future of Hospitals. World Economic Forum. Davos (2019), available at www.youtube.com.

58. www.jefferson.edu.

59. Bertini and Koenigsberg. The Ends Game. How smart companies stop selling products and start delivering value. (2020) The MIT Press.

60. Timothy Aungst. The Startups Disrupting the Pharmacy Sector - 2020 Wrap-Up. (2020) 29 Nov, available at www. thedigitalapothecary.com.

61. 10 Disruptive Technologies That Will Transform Pharma. The Medical Futurist. (2016) 10 Aug, available at https:// medicalfuturist.com.

62. Eric Sagonowsky. At $475,000, is Novartis' Kymriah a bargain—
or another example of skyrocketing prices? FIERCE pharma
(2017) 31 Aug, www.fiercepharma.com.

63. www.hcp.novartis.com/products/kymriah/.

64. Joshua Cohen. At Over $2 Million Zolgensma is the World's
Most Expensive Therapy, yet Relatively Cost-Effective. Forbes
(2019) 5 June, www.forbes.com.

65. www.zolgensma.com.

66. WMA Declaration of Helsinki — Ethical Principles for Medical
Research Involving Human Subjects. www.wma.net.

67. www.spacex.com.

68. Space Investor Steve Jurvetson on Studio 1.0. (2016) 4 Oct,
available at www.youtube.com.

69. SpaceX and Why they are Daring to Think Big | Investor Steve
Jurvetson. (2015) 28 Jan, available at www.youtube.com.

70. https://en.wikipedia.org/wiki/SpaceX.

71. Anna Heiney. SpaceX Demo-2 Will Showcase Public-Private
Partnership Benefits. NASA commercial crew program (2020)
7 May, available at www.blogs.nasa.gov.

72. NIH to launch public-private partnership to speed COVID-19
vaccine and treatment options. (2020) 17 Apr, available at
www.nih.gov.

73. Sharon LaFraniere et al. Politics, Science and the Remarkable
Race for a Coronavirus Vaccine. New York Times (2020) 21
Nov, available at www.nytimes.com.

74. Accelerating COVID-19 Therapeutic Interventions and
Vaccines (ACTIV), available at www.nih.gov.

75. Margaret A. Tempero. NCCN Guidelines Updates: Pancreatic
Cancer. JNCCN (2019) online publication May, available at
jnncn.org.

76. www.pancreaticcancereurope.eu.

77. www.amractionfund.com.

CHAPTER 3 – Applying value-based principles to redesign a patient-centered health system

78. www.diabetesatlas.org.

79. Verena Voelter and Hanna Boëthius. Focus on the Patient – the Rest will Follow. Available at www.verena-voelter.medium. com.

80. Clayton M. Christensen et al. What Customers Want from Your Products. (2006) Harvard Business School Working Knowledge, available at https://hbswk.hbs.edu/.

81. Joanne Lynn et al. Value-Based Payments Require Valuing What Matters to Patients. JAMA (2015); 314(14):1445-6.

82. Better ways to pay for health care. OECD (2016) June, available at www.oecd.org.

83. Robert Kaplan. How to Pay for Health Care Delivery: Bundled Payments and Time-Driven Activity-Based Costing on the Move. VBHC Thinkers Magazine. (2019) Aug, p. 8, available at www.vbhc.nl.

84. Michael E. Porter and Elizabeth Olmsted Teisberg. Redefining Health Care. Creating Value-Based Competition on Results (2006) Harvard Business Press.

85. Michael E. Porter and Thomas H Lee. The strategy that will fix healthcare. Harvard Business Review Magazine (2013) Oct.

86. Michael E. Porter and Mark R. Kramer. Creating Shared Value. Harvard Business Review Magazine (2011) Jan-Feb.

87. OSH/investor relations presentation Q4 (2020); available at www.oakstreethealth.com.

88. Michael E. Porter et al. Oak Street Health: Value-Based Primary Care. Harvard Business School Case (2017) 717-437 (revised April 2018).

89. Griffin Myers. VBHC Thinkers Magazine (2020) Special Edition, May, p. 14, available at www.vbhc.nl

90. More effective and patient centered care. OECD library, available at www.oecd-ilibrary.org.

91. www.diabeter.nl.

92. Christer Mjåset et al. Value-Based Health Care in Four Different Health Care Systems. (2020) www.catalyst.nejm.org.

93. Michael E. Porter. Value-Based Health Care Delivery. Harvard Business School Partners Healthcare Value Based Health Care Seminar. (2014) 15 Jan, available at www.isc.hbs.edu.

94. www.parkinsonnet.com.

95. Fred van Eenennaam. The resilience of the Dutch Healthcare System. (2020) Nov 13, available at www.youtube.com.

96. 4. Comprehensive Medical Evaluation and Assessment of Comorbidities: Standards of Medical Care in Diabetes – 2021 by the American Diabetes Association. Diabetes Care (2021) Jan; 44(Supplement 1):S40-S52.

97. Joint Value – VBHC Prize 2020 Nominee Pitch. (2020) 13 Nov, available on www.youtube.com.

98. www.ichom.org.

99. Michael E. Porter et al. Standardizing Patient Outcomes Measurements. N Eng J Med (2016); 374:504-506.

100. www.nordichealth2030.org.

101. Programa Contigo - VBHC Prize 2020 Nominee Pitch. (2020) 13 Nov, available on www.youtube.com.

102. www.GoInvo.com/vision/determinants-of-health/.

103. David McDaid et al (ed). Promoting Health, Preventing Disease. The economic case. OECD publishing (2015).

104. Ana Paula Beck da Silva Etges et al. A standardized framework to evaluate the quality of studies using TDABC in healthcare: the TDABC in Healthcare Consortium Consensus Statement. BMC Health Services Research (2020) 20:1107.

CHAPTER 4 – Acquiring a digital footprint to eliminate inefficiencies and foster cooperation

105. Eric Topol. Deep Medicine. (2019) Basic Books, New York.

106. Matt Novak. Telemedicine Predicted in 1925. Smithsonian Magazine (2012) 14 Mar.

107. Tracey A Lustig. The role of telehealth in an evolving healthcare environment. Workshop summary. (2012) The Institute of Medicine of National Academies. The national academic press.

108. Tackling Wasteful Spending on Health. OECD (2017). OECD Publishing, Paris, available at www.oecd.org/els/health-systems.

109. State Of Healthcare Report: Investment & Sector Trends to Watch. CB Insights (2020), available at www.cbinsights.com.

110. Marius Mainz. The Characterization of Digital Health in Scientific Research: A Bibliometric Analysis (2020); personal communication.

111. Adam S. Miner et al. Chatbots in the fight against the COVID-19 pandemic. npj Digital Medicine (2020) 3:65.

112. Choi Moon-Hee. Seoul National University Hospital Using LG Robots to Combat COVID-19. (2020) 25 Mar, available at www.businesskorea.co.kr.

113. www.ada.com.

114. www.babylonhealth.com/us.

115. www.owkin.com.

116. Thomas Clozel in #LetsTalkValue in Health Care, podcast #8, available at https://5phealthcaresolutions.com/podcast.html.

117. www.substra.ai/en/healthchain-project.

118. www.melloddy.eu.

119. Deep learning-based classification of mesothelioma improves prediction of patient outcome. Nature Medicine (2019); 25:1519–1525.

120. A better AI-based tool for mesothelioma. Nature Reviews Clinical Oncology (2019);16, p. 722.

121. A deep learning model to predict RNA-Seq expression of tumours from whole slide images. Nature Communications (2020); (11)3877.

122. Jenni Spinner. Current Health: RPM can help clear COVID-19 challenges. Outsourcing-pharma.com Newsletter (2020) 30 Sep.

123. Chronic Diseases in America, available at www.cdc.gov.

124. Hugh Waters et al. Chronic diseases are taxing our health care system and our economy. STAT News (2018) 31 May.

125. Friedrich Koehler et al. Efficacy of telemedical interventional management in patients with heart failure (TIM-HF2): a randomised, controlled, parallel-group, unmasked trial. Lancet (2018); 392:1047–57.

126. Anne Sig Vestergaard et al. Is telehealthcare for heart failure patients cost-effective? An economic evaluation alongside the Danish TeleCare North heart failure trial. BMJ Open (2020); 10:e031670.

127. Be-Optilys information available at www.be-ys-health-solutions.com.

128. Rahul Varshneya. How AI is streamlining physician workflows. Health Europa, Research & Innovation News (2021) 5 Jan, available at healtheuropa.eu.

129. Deeksha M. Shama et al. DeepBreath: Diagnostsic Pattern Detection for COVID-19 in Digital Lung Auscultations. In print (2021) available at www.epfl.ch.

130. Yazeed Zoabi et al. Machine learning-based prediction of COVID-19 diagnosis based on symptoms. npj Digital Medicine (2021); 4:3.

131. Dave Muoio. Israeli AI model predicts COVID-19 cases among

general population using self-reported symptoms. (2021) 6 Jan, available at www.mobihealthnews.com.

132. Discover the new technology managing cancer symptoms for patients. Health Europa, Research & Innovation News (2021) 11 Jan.

133. Outcomes4Me Raises $4.7 Million to Help Patients Navigate Cancer Care Using AI, available at www.outcomes4me.com/news.

134. Alexander Pinker. Smart Hospital – how the University Hospital in Essen is shaping the future of medicine. Medialist Innovation. (2020) 16 Feb.

135. Das erste Smart Hospital Deutschlands. YouTube (2018) 17 Jul, available at www.youtube.com.

136. The SPARC Innovation Program at Mayo Clinic. Transforming the patient care experience through research and innovation, available at www.vol10.cases.som.yale.edu.

137. www.centerforinnovation.mayo.edu.

138. Laura Dyrda. Mayo Clinic bets big on digital transformation, to reinvest 'hundreds of millions' in the next decade. BECKERS HEALTH IT newsletter (2020) 2 Mar.

139. Daniel Cohen et al. Healthtech in the fast lane: What is fueling investor excitement? (2020) 1 Dec, available at www.mckinsey.com.

140. From Wearable Sensors to Smart Implants – Toward Pervasive and Personalized Healthcare. Transactions on Biomedical Engineering. (2015); 62(12) 2750-2762.

141. Digital Health Market Size to Hit Around US$ 833.44 bn by 2027. (2020) 17 Nov, available at globenewswire.com.

142. FDA Launches the Digital Health Center of Excellence. (2020) 22 Sep, available at www.fda.gov.

143. Stan Benjamens et al. The state of artificial intelligence-based

FDA-approved medical devices and algorithms: an online database. npj Digital Medicine (2020); 3:118.

144. AI Algorithm May Help Monitor Parkinson's Severity Remotely, Study Suggests. (2020) 13 Aug, available at www.parkisonsnewstoday.com.

145. Khaligh-Razavi et al. A self-administered, artificial intelligence (AI) platform for cognitive assessment in multiple sclerosis (MS). BMC Neurology (2020) 20:193.

146. FDA Approves Video Game Based on UCSF Brain Research as ADHD Therapy for Kids. (2020) 15 Jun, available at www.ucsf.edu/news.

147. www.sleepio.com.

148. Colin A. Espie et al. A Randomized, Placebo-Controlled Trial of Online Cognitive Behavioral Therapy for Chronic Insomnia Disorder Delivered via an Automated Media-Rich Web Application. Sleep. (2012); 35(6):769–781.

149. Christopher M. Barnes et al. Helping employees sleep well: Effects of cognitive behavioral therapy for insomnia on work outcomes. Journal of Applied Psychology (2017); 102(1),104-113.

150. Emer R. McGrath. Sleep to lower elevated blood pressure: study protocol for a randomized controlled trial. Trials (2014); 15:393.

151. www.bfarm.de/EN/MedicalDevices/DIGA.

152. Spahn Digital die Letzte: DVPMG-Entwurf liegt vor. (2020) 26 Nov, available at www.e-health-com.de.

153. Adherence to Long-Term Therapies – Evidence for Action. World Health Organization (2003).

154. Marie T. Brown et al. Medication adherence: WHO cares? Mayo Clin Proc. (2011); 86(4):304-314.

155. Lars Osterberg et al. Adherence to medication. N Engl J Med (2005); 353(5):487-497.

156. www.collabree.com.

157. www.clinicaltrial.gov.

158. Orel O. Luga et al. Adherence and health care costs. Risk Manag Healthc Policy. (2014); 7:35-44.

159. Meera Viswanathan M et al. Interventions to Improve Adherence to Self-administered Medications for Chronic Diseases in the United States: A Systematic Review. Ann Intern Med. (2012); 157(11):785-795.

160. European Commission; OECD. Health at a Glance: Europe 2018 – State of Health in the EU Cycle. (2018).

161. Magazin D, Krankenversicherer DS. Santésuisse. (2012) 6 Dec, available at www.santesuisse.ch.

162. Madeleine Hillyer. How has technology changed – and changed us – in the past 20 years? Pioneers of Change Summit, WEF. (2020) 18 Nov, available at www.wef.org.

163. Javier Andreu-Perez et al. Hospitals in England to receive funding for digital prescribing. Health Europa, Research & Innovation News. (2020) 18 Nov.

164. Opening of the Danish Medicines Agency's Data Analytics Centre. (2020) 16 Nov, available at www.healthcaredenmark. dk.

165. Jesper Kjær. Director of Division, Data Analytics Center (DAC). Video available at https://vimeo.com/481450857.

166. Morten Schmidt et al. The Danish health care system and epidemiological research: from health care contacts to database records. Clin Epidemiol. (2019); 11:563-591.

167. Katrin Rupalla, Personal communication in the context of *#LetsTalkValue in Health Care*, podcast #3, available at https://5phealthcaresolutions.com/podcast.html.

168. Digital Health Index, available at www.bertelsmann-stiftung.de/ en.

169. www.e-estonia.com.

170. www. knowledge4policy.ec.europa.eu/home_en.

171. eHealth: Digital health and care. Available at ec.europa.eu/ health/ehealth/home_en.

172. Florin Zubașcu. New €5.1B health programme due to start in 2021. Science Business® (2020) 15 Dec, available at www. sciencebusiness.net.

173. Pharmaceutical Strategy for Europe (2020) 25 Nov, available at ec.europa.eu.

174. Global digital health ecosystem global report (2020) 5 Jan, available at www.julien-desalaberry-medium.com.

175. NHS saves around £75m a year thanks to historic public sector data network migration. NHS digital (2020) 13 Nov, available at www.digital.nhs.uk.

176. Matthias Becker et al. How Digital Divides Health Care Providers. The Boston Consulting Group (2020) 17 Dec, available at www.bcg.com.

177. Yoni Goldwasser. Will AI Replace Our Doctors? (2020) 17 Nov, available at www.medium.com.

178. Shivan Bhavnani et al. Physicians will decide the fate of the digital therapeutics industry. Mobihealthnews (2020) 20 Nov, available at www.mobihealthnews.com.

179. Fortschritt bei Rahmenbedingungen, Nachholbedarf bei praktischen Anwendungen. E-Health Monitor Report (2020) 12 Nov, available at www.mckinsey.de.

CHAPTER 5 – Adopting a playbook for multi-party collaboration to catalyze change behavior

180. Martin Luther King Jr in a sermon called "Loving Your Enemies", delivered at the Dexter Avenue Baptist Church in Montgomery, Alabama (December 25, 1957).

181. Creating Value in Integrative Negotiations: Myth of the Fixed-Pie of Resources. The Negotiation Newsletter, Harvard University. (2020) 24 Sep, available at pon.harvard.edu/ tagnegotiation-newsletter/.

182. Vanessa Candeias, *#LetsTalkValue in Health Care*, podcast #9, available at https://5phealthcaresolutions.com/podcast.html.

183. Vanessa Candeias et al. Collaborating for Healthy Living: From Bottlenecks to Solutions. (2014) available at www.weforum.org.

184. www.pon.harvard.edu.

185. Roger Fisher et al. Getting to YES. Negotiating agreement without giving in. (1981) Penguin.

186. Katherine Shronk (ed). What is Negotiation? The Negotiation Newsletter, Harvard University. (2020) 2 Nov, available at pon. harvard.edu/tagnegotiation-newsletter/.

187. www.rebuildcongress.org.

188. Charles Barker in Harvard Heritage, available on www. primemover.co.

189. Bruce Patten. Understanding dispute resolution processes – Negotiation. In: The Handbook of Dispute Resolution. A publication of the Program on Negotiation (PON) at Harvard Law School. (2005) (ed. Michael L Moffitt et al) Jossey-Bass, a Wiley Imprint.

190. Jonathan Hughes et al. What's Your Negotiation Strategy? (2020) Harvard Business Review Magazine Jul-Aug.

191. Bruce Patten. The Sunday Minute at the Negotiation Newsletter. (2021) 10 Jan, available at pon.harvard.edu/ tagnegotiation-newsletter/.

192. William Ury. Getting past No. Negotiating in difficult situations. (1991) Bantam books.

193. Robert Mnookin. The Sunday Minute at the Negotiation Newsletter. (2020) 25 Oct, available at pon.harvard.edu/ tagnegotiation-newsletter/.

194. Commencement address delivered by Steve Jobs, CEO of Apple Computer and of Pixar Animation Studios. (2005) Jun 12, available at www.news.standford.edu.

195. Kessely Hong. The Sunday Minute at the Negotiation Newsletter. (2020) 19 Jul, available at pon.harvard.edu/tagnegotiation-newsletter/.

196. Jesùs San Miguel et al. Pomalidomide plus low-dose dexamethasone versus high-dose dexamethasone alone for patients with relapsed and refractory multiple myeloma (MM-003): a randomised, open-label, phase 3 trial. Lancet Oncol (2013); 14(11):1055-1066.

CONCLUSION – Bringing it all together in a collaborative, value-based and smart *Tango for Five*

197. Yuval Noah Harari. This is the nature of emergencies. They fast-forward historical processes. Financial Times (2020) 20 Mar.

198. Amanda Gorman. Youth Poet Amanda Gorman Recites Poem at Presidential Inauguration. (2021), 20 Jan, available at www.youtube.com.

199. Hanna Boëthius, *#LetsTalkValue in Health Care*, podcast #1, available at https://5phealthcaresolutions.com/podcast.html.

200. www.hannaboethius.com.

201. Pascal Deschaseaux, *#LetsTalkValue in Health Care*, podcast #4, available at https://5phealthcaresolutions.com/podcast.html.

202. Richard G. Hamermesh et al. Intermountain Healthcare: Pursuing Precision Medicine. Harvard Business School Case Collection (2017), available at www.hbs.edu.

203. Lindsay R. Resnick. Trends Relevant in Healthcare Before COVID-19 Will Remain So After. Managed

Healthcare Executive (2020) 21 Apr, available at www. managedhealthcareexecutive.com.

204. Davos Agenda: What you need to know about the future of global health. (2021) 24 Jan, available at www.weforum.org.

205. Mohamed Kande et al. Don't Fear AI. It Will Lead To Long-Term Job Growth. Forbes (2020) 26 Oct, available at www.forbes. com.

206. The Future of Jobs Report 2020. (2020) 20 Oct, available at www.weforum.org.

207. Closing the Skills Gap: Key Insights and Success Metrics. White paper (2020) 30 Nov, available at www.weforum.org.

208. Adam Brandenburger et al. The Rules of Co-opetition. Harvard Business Review Magazine (2021) Jan-Feb, p. 49.

209. Michael E. Porter. The Five Competitive Forces That Shape Strategy. Harvard Business Review (2008) Jan, available at www.hbr.org.

210. Patrick Noack. The Fifth Industrial Revolution: where mind meets machine. The National US (2020) 9 Aug, available at thenationalnews.com.

Supplemental material

211. Aledade. Assessing Your Goals and Objectives for Value-Based Care, White Paper, available at www.resources.aledade. com.

212. Anjali Nursimulu. Value Creation in Precision Medicine. Acknowledging the need to devise new ways to measure the value of healthcare. (2019) 11 Dec, available at www.epfl.ch.

213. EIT Health. Implementing value-based health care in Europe: Handbook for pioneers. Director Gregory Katz. (2020).

214. Karin Frick et al. NEXT HEALTH. Einfacher durch das Ökosystem der Gesundheit. Gottlieb Duttweiler Institute (2020), available at www.gdi.ch.

215. Health 2030 – Federal Council's health policy strategy 2020–2030, available at www.bag.admin.ch.

216. Multistakeholder Collaboration for Healthy Living Toolkit for Joint Action. (2013) 17 Jan, available at www.weforum.org.

217. Precision Medicine Readiness Principles Resource Guide: Innovation loop. (2020) 1 Oct, available at www.weforum.org.

SUPPLEMENTARY MATERIALS

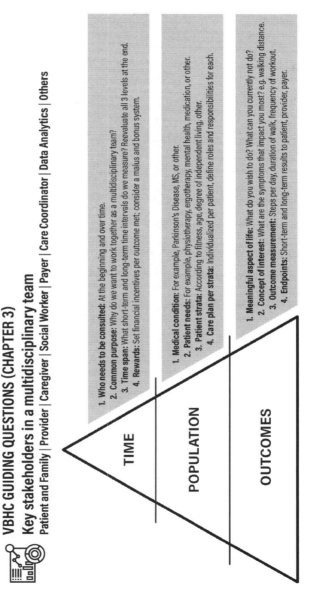

VBHC GUIDING QUESTIONS (CHAPTER 3)
Key stakeholders in a multidisciplinary team
Patient and Family | Provider | Caregiver | Social Worker | Payer | Care Coordinator | Data Analytics | Others

TIME

1. **Who needs to be consulted:** At the beginning and over time.
2. **Common purpose:** Why do we want to work together as a multidisciplinary team?
3. **Time span:** What short-term and long-term time intervals do we measure? Reevaluate all 3 levels at the end.
4. **Rewards:** Set financial incentives per outcome met; consider a malus and bonus system.

POPULATION

1. **Medical condition:** For example, Parkinson's Disease, MS, or other.
2. **Patient needs:** For example, physiotherapy, ergotherapy, mental health, medication, or other.
3. **Patient strata:** According to fitness, age, degree of independent living, other.
4. **Care plan per strata:** Individualized per patient, define roles and responsibilities for each.

OUTCOMES

1. **Meaningful aspect of life:** What do you wish to do? What can you currently not do?
2. **Concept of interest:** What are the symptoms that impact you most? e.g. walking distance.
3. **Outcome measurement:** Steps per day, duration of walk, frequency of workout.
4. **Endpoints:** Short-term and long-term results to patient, provider, payer.

Sources: TDABC in Healthcare Consortium Consensus Statement [104]; Diabeter OSH care team models [87,91]

5P GUIDING QUESTIONS

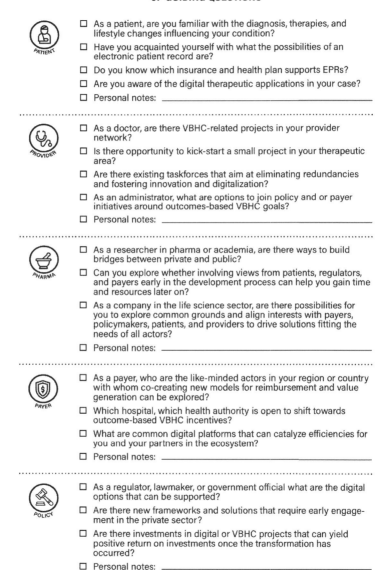

PATIENT

☐ As a patient, are you familiar with the diagnosis, therapies, and lifestyle changes influencing your condition?

☐ Have you acquainted yourself with what the possibilities of an electronic patient record are?

☐ Do you know which insurance and health plan supports EPRs?

☐ Are you aware of the digital therapeutic applications in your case?

☐ Personal notes: _____

PROVIDER

☐ As a doctor, are there VBHC-related projects in your provider network?

☐ Is there opportunity to kick-start a small project in your therapeutic area?

☐ Are there existing taskforces that aim at eliminating redundancies and fostering innovation and digitalization?

☐ As an administrator, what are options to join policy and or payer initiatives around outcomes-based VBHC goals?

☐ Personal notes: _____

PHARMA

☐ As a researcher in pharma or academia, are there ways to build bridges between private and public?

☐ Can you explore whether involving views from patients, regulators, and payers early in the development process can help you gain time and resources later on?

☐ As a company in the life science sector, are there possibilities for you to explore common grounds and align interests with payers, policymakers, patients, and providers to drive solutions fitting the needs of all actors?

☐ Personal notes: _____

PAYER

☐ As a payer, who are the like-minded actors in your region or country with whom co-creating new models for reimbursement and value generation can be explored?

☐ Which hospital, which health authority is open to shift towards outcome-based VBHC incentives?

☐ What are common digital platforms that can catalyze efficiencies for you and your partners in the ecosystem?

☐ Personal notes: _____

POLICY

☐ As a regulator, lawmaker, or government official what are the digital options that can be supported?

☐ Are there new frameworks and solutions that require early engagement in the private sector?

☐ Are there investments in digital or VBHC projects that can yield positive return on investments once the transformation has occurred?

☐ Personal notes: _____

Made in the USA
Monee, IL
03 May 2021

acbcd504-108b-4c40-89cd-ba54a9358626R01